James Gunson Lawn

Mine Accounts and Mining Book-Keeping

A Manual for the Use of Students, Managers of Metalliferous Mines and Collieries, and

Others Interested in Mining

James Gunson Lawn

Mine Accounts and Mining Book-Keeping
A Manual for the use of Students, Managers of Metalliferous Mines and Collieries, and Others Interested in Mining

ISBN/EAN: 9783743395220

Manufactured in Europe, USA, Canada, Australia, Japa

Cover: Foto ©Andreas Hilbeck / pixelio.de

Manufactured and distributed by brebook publishing software (www.brebook.com)

James Gunson Lawn

Mine Accounts and Mining Book-Keeping

MINE ACCOUNTS

AND

MINING BOOK-KEEPING:

*A MANUAL FOR THE USE OF STUDENTS,
MANAGERS OF METALLIFEROUS MINES AND COLLIERIES,
AND OTHERS INTERESTED IN MINING.*

BY

JAMES GUNSON LAWN,
A. R. S. M.,
ASSOCIATE MEMBER OF THE INSTITUTION OF CIVIL ENGINEERS; FELLOW OF THE GEOLOGICAL SOCIETY;
MEMBER OF THE NORTH OF ENGLAND AND AMERICAN INSTITUTES OF MINING ENGINEERS;
PROFESSOR OF MINING, ETC., AT THE SOUTH AFRICAN SCHOOL OF MINES.

WITH NUMEROUS EXAMPLES FROM THE ACTUAL PRACTICE
OF LEADING MINING COMPANIES.

LONDON:
CHARLES GRIFFIN & COMPANY, LIMITED;
EXETER STREET, STRAND.
1897.

PREFACE.

THIS book is the outcome of a short course of Lectures on MINE ACCOUNTS delivered at the Royal College of Science, London.

Both the lectures and the book were suggested by Dr. Le Neve Foster, who, in spite of numerous and urgent duties, has given me most valuable aid in preparing the present treatise.

In getting together materials I have been generously assisted by many friends. In addition to the acknowledgments made in footnotes, I would especially thank Mr. Bedford M'Neill, A.R.S.M., and Mr. T. H. Everett for kindly criticism and help.

Chapter X. has been carefully revised by Mr. Alfred Smart, of the firm of Messrs. W. F. Smart & Son, Chartered Accountants; and Mr. L. H. Cooke, A.R.S.M., has rendered important service in reading the proofs.

I would impress upon the student that the book-keeping forms employed must always be thoroughly adapted to the circumstances of each individual mine. Although the illustrative examples are numerous, and have been taken, almost invariably, from actual practice, yet they must only be looked upon as suggestive, and must not be rigidly copied without considering whether some modification should not be introduced to meet the requirements of the particular case in point.

JAMES G. LAWN.

KIMBERLEY, 1897.

CONTENTS.

INTRODUCTION.

	PAGE		PAGE
Reasons for Keeping Mining Accounts connected with—		2. The Owner,	2
		3. The Safety of Workmen,	3
1. Actual Working of a Mine,	1	4. The Country at large,	3

PART I.—ENGAGEMENT AND PAYMENT OF WORKMEN.

Chapter I.—Engagement of Workmen and Period between Pay-Days.

Engagement of Workmen, . . . 4 | Period between Pay-days, . . . 11

Chapter II.—Data Determining Gross Amount Due to Workmen.

A. Length of Time Worked,	12	Exploitation,	15
Overtime,	12	Sliding Scales,	20
B. Amount of Work done,	14	Modifications,	20
Sinking and Driving,	14	C. Value of Mineral gotten,	21

Chapter III.—Deductions.

A. Wages Determined by Time Worked, 22 | C. Wages Determined by Value of
B. ,, by Amount of Work done, 25 | Mineral gotten, ... 26

Chapter IV.—Pay-Sheets, Due-Bills, and Pay-Tickets.

Pay-sheets, ... 26 | Due-bills and Pay-tickets, . 30

PART II.—PURCHASES AND SALES.

Chapter V.—Purchase and Distribution of Stores.

Stores,	35	B. Books and Forms Relating to Receipt and Distribution,	40
A. Books and Forms Relating to Purchase,	36	Receipt of Stores,	40
Requisitions,	36	Distribution of Stores,	41
Quotations and Contracts,	36	C. Books connected with Balancing Stores used, and Stock,	44
Orders,	38		
Invoices and Payment of Accounts,	38	Stock-taking,	46

Chapter VI.—Sales of Product.

Methods of Sale,	47	Tin Ore,	49
Contract,	47	Coal,	49
Tender,	47	Silver Ore,	53
Delivery of, and Payment for, Mineral,	49	Gold Ore,	55

PART III.—WORKING SUMMARIES AND ANALYSES.

Chapter VII.—Summaries of Minerals Raised, Dressed, and Sold; and of Labour.

	PAGE		PAGE
Summaries, .	57	Labour Analyses, .	66

Chapter VIII.—Analyses of Costs.

First Method, . .	68	Second Method, . .	74

Chapter IX.—Accounts forwarded to Head Office.

Case A—Where Vouchers are sent:		Sales of Product, ...	77
Salaries and Wages Paid, . . .	77	Cash Account, ...	77
Purchases, Consumption, and Stocks		Ore Raised and Treated, . .	77
of Stores, ...	77	Case B—Where Vouchers are not sent,	77

PART IV.—LEDGER, BALANCE SHEET, AND COMPANY BOOKS.

Chapter X.—Head Office Books.

Ledger, ...	79	Bills Receivable and Payable Account,	84
Principal Accounts of a Mining Company,	80	Discount and Interest Account, .	85
Capital Account, ...	81	Product Account, ...	85
Sale and Purchase Accounts, . .	82	Working Accounts, ...	86
Capital Expenditure, . . .	82	Profit and Loss Account, . .	86
Personal, ...	83	Journal, ...	87
Stores, ...	83	Inventory, ...	90
Wages Account, ...	83	Balance Sheet, ...	90
Bad Debts Account, ...	83	Example, ...	91
Cash Account, ...	83	Bibliography, ...	102

Chapter XI.—Redemption of Capital.

Redemption of Capital, . . .	103	C. By Annual Sum depending on	
1. Debentures, ...	104	Mineral worked, . . .	106
2. Sinking Fund, ...	104	3. Enlarged Dividends or Bonuses, .	106
A. By Equal Annual Sums, .	104	Depreciation, ...	109
B. By Annual Sum varying accord-		Reserve Fund, ...	110
ing to a Formula, . .	105	Bibliography, ...	110

Chapter XII.—General Considerations and Companies Books.

Private Individuals, ...	111	Books connected with Shares, . .	119
Private Partnership Companies, .	112	Allotment Book, ...	119
References, ...	113	Transfer Receipt Book, . . .	119
Cost-book Companies, . . .	113	List of Transfers, ...	120
References, ...	116	Shares Certificate Book, . . .	120
Limited Liability Companies, . .	116	Guard Book for Transfers, . .	120
Stocks and Shares, ...	117	Miscellaneous Books, . . .	120
Debentures, ...	118	Bibliography, ...	120

CONTENTS. ix

PART V.—REPORTS AND STATISTICS.

Chapter XIII.—Reports of Inspections of Workings and Machinery.

	PAGE		PAGE
A. Colliery Reports, &c.,	122	Permits to fire Shots and carry Safety Lamp Key,	125
Inspections,	122	B. Ore Mine Reports, &c.,	125
Report Books,	123	C. Miscellaneous Reports, &c.,	126
Measurement of Ventilating Current,	124		

Chapter XIV.—Reports of Mining Companies.

Managers' Reports,	129	Reports of Directors,	133
Diagrams,	130	Reports of Cost-book Mines,	134
Tabular Statements,	130		

Chapter XV.—Mining Statistics.

Great Britain, ... 137 | Other Countries, . . 141

BIBLIOGRAPHY, ... 144

INDEX, ... 145

INTRODUCTION.

For the purposes of this book we shall interpret the term "Mine Accounts" widely, and shall include all the books and forms used about a mine, or in connection with Mining Companies, whether they deal with quantities or not, and also Mining Statistics, as being mine accounts in a larger sense; as, however, we are writing primarily for mining students, those books and forms which belong more peculiarly to the province of the secretary of a company will be treated with greater brevity than those which more directly concern the mine manager.

Certain accounts are required by law, and compliance with statutory obligations is not a matter of choice; attention will be drawn, as we proceed, to various clauses in British Acts of Parliament which bear on Mine Accounts.

The importance of a good system of book-keeping to a mine owner can scarcely be over-estimated. This will at once be apparent if we consider briefly some of the reasons for keeping mine accounts. They may be arranged under four heads—viz., those connected with—

    1. The actual working of a mine.
    2. The owner.*
    3. The safety of workmen.
    4. The country at large.

1. **Reasons Connected with the Actual Working of a Mine.**—It is necessary to keep accounts in order that the relations of the employer and employed may be correctly regulated. Certain monies are due periodically to the workmen for their labour, reckoned by the number of days worked or amount of mineral got, or, generally, for services rendered in some way; while certain amounts are owed by the men for materials supplied, rent of cottages, sick club, and so on. The net amount due to the men must be calculated before each pay-day, and set out in proper form, so that every explanation of the exact state of their account can be given to them on the pay-day, or preferably a day or two before.

Again, for working a mine various kinds of stores and materials are required; these have to be bought from various merchants; and, further, the product of the mine has to be sold, possibly in comparatively small quantities regularly disposed of to the same buyer, as in the case of gold, or perhaps in large quantities sold to a hundred different people, as in the case of coal. All these transactions should be recorded, not only that their influence on the profit or loss of working may be ascertained, but that payments may be made regularly, monies due collected, and the general relations of the mine with these buyers and sellers kept straight.

As the stores and materials used at a mine often constitute a very

---

*By "owner" is meant the individual or partnership financially responsible for the working of a mine.

important item of expenditure, their consumption must be carefully watched, and an exact account kept of everything delivered to the workmen. It is also necessary to keep an exact account of the quantity of mineral raised and of the quantity treated by dressing operations, although these accounts may not be necessary in connection with the payment of workmen, in order to determine the efficiency of the mining plant, and to arrange the sales.

Finally, careful summaries and analyses of the cost of each stage of production of the saleable mineral, and of other necessary costs not directly connected with production, should be made weekly, or fortnightly, or monthly, so that the manager may be able to ascertain the proportion which each bears to the total cost, to learn where it is possible to economise, and, generally, to conduct the working in an efficient manner.

2. **Reasons Connected with the Owner.**—The owner is chiefly interested in finding out, quickly and accurately, whether the result of any period of work has been profit or loss; and also, exactly why it falls out that profit or loss, as the case may be, has resulted; in other words, there must be complete and accurate data, from which a balance sheet—and summaries and analyses of mineral wrought and dressed, of product sold, and of all expenditure—can be drawn up.

The gross profit or loss might, indeed, be arrived at without any system of accounts at all. If, at the beginning of a period, an inventory were made of all the assets of a company—mine and plant, cash in hand, money to be received; stock of ore, stores, and materials; and from the total sum, the amount of monies owing were subtracted—the financial position of the concern at that point of time would be determined. Then, if, at the end of the period, the same process were gone through, the resulting sum, if greater than that arrived at for the beginning of the period, would indicate a gain as the result of that period of work; but if less, a loss, to the extent of the difference, would be shown. Nevertheless, only with great labour could a result, in any degree accurate, be arrived at by this method; and even then it would not be of much value, for the bare fact of profit or loss is not sufficient information either for the owner or for the manager of a mine.

If a profit has resulted, it is necessary to know exactly how it has happened; and whether it is a sign of careful and skilful management, or whether it ought to have been greater; for there may be a profit in spite of wasteful methods of mining and treating the mineral, and excessive office and other expenses; in fact, instead of indicating good management, the profit may be due to the natural richness of the mine, and may have accrued in spite of mismanagement.

If a loss is shown, the owner should be informed how it has occurred; whether it is due to scarcity or poverty of the mineral, or to heavy expenses in mining and dressing, or to carriage, or stores, or royalty, or office expenses, so that he may decide whether the obstacles in the way of profitable mining are insurmountable or not.

Further, to understand his position fully, the owner should receive, in addition, periodical reports of the condition of the mine and its future prospects.

Very frequently a mine is situated at a great distance from the chief office of the owner, and although it is not necessary that every detail connected with working be sent home, yet full summarised accounts of all expenditure and receipts, of results of working, and of the state of the property must be forwarded.

In the case of companies owning mines, again, there are often numerous shareholders; this necessitates a number of books, in order that a careful record of the shareholders may be kept, the transfer of shares carried out, and dividends paid or calls made.

Finally, experience has shown that it is desirable to have means of knowing that each man employed duly performs the work allotted to him. In this connection accounts are of the utmost importance. For, by means of proper records, the foremen have a check on the men—supposing, of course, that they know what length of time a particular piece of work requires—the manager controls the foremen, and also the storekeeper and other officials; and, in the case of a company, the interests of the shareholders are safeguarded by the auditors.

3. **Reasons Connected with the Safety of Workmen.**—Experience has proved that careful and frequent inspection of underground workings, of engines, and of plant generally is one means of guarding against accidents, which are sadly too frequent in connection with mines. As a guarantee that such inspections have been made, careful records signed by the persons responsible are necessary, and these reports must be readily accessible to those interested.

4. **Reasons Connected with the Country at Large.**—Mines are not merely of personal and local interest, but are undertakings of national importance; and further, in most countries the working of mines is regulated by law. Hence, it is important that "accurate and timely statistics," relating to the mining industry of a country, should be published; and in order that the details from a particular mine may be forwarded to the deputed authority without delay at the end of the particular period to which they relate, it is evident that a good system of accounts must be employed.

All these requirements must be fulfilled with the greatest amount of clearness attainable, without undue complexity in the methods and books used, and without unnecessary labour, which would mean not only increased expense, but increased likelihood of error. The latter must be further guarded against by arranging that the various books check each other. This internal check of the accuracy of the books must not be confused with the check upon the general working of the mine, although it, too, helps to prevent fraud,—in the office,—as well as to ensure the accuracy of the records. To attain these ends, orderliness must be pushed to an extreme, and no pains spared in designing a set of books and forms which shall be thoroughly adapted to the circumstances of each particular case.

In treating the subject the following order will be adopted :—

I. Books and Forms connected with the Engagement and Payment of Workmen.
II. Books and Forms connected with Purchases and Sales.
III. Working Analyses and Summaries.
IV. Head-Office Books, including Balance Sheet and Company's Books.
V. Reports and Statistics.

PART I.

ENGAGEMENT AND PAYMENT OF WORKMEN.

CHAPTER I.—ENGAGEMENT OF WORKMEN AND PERIOD BETWEEN PAY-DAYS.

Engagement of Workmen.—In England men are usually engaged by the mine-manager or the under-agent. In the case of some mines, there is no sort of formality whatever, the names of new hands being simply entered in the books of the mine according to their work. At others, the men sign an agreement, in accordance with the provisions of the Truck Acts,* allowing certain deductions from their wages, though, by section 3 of the new law of 1896, this agreement in writing is no longer necessary, provided that the terms of the contract are contained in a notice kept constantly posted up in some place where it can be easily seen and read by the workmen. If there is a formal agreement, it is usually printed on the front page of a book, or on the top of each page, with columns underneath for the signatures of the workmen and witnesses, and for other details. The following will suffice as an example :—

THE................COLLIERY COMPANY, LIMITED.

......................COLLIERIES.

WE, THE UNDERSIGNED, being respectively persons employed by The.....................Colliery Company, Limited, do hereby severally and respectively agree and contract with the said Company, that the said Company may, from time to time, out of any wages earned by us respectively, and payable by the said Company, stop, or deduct, all and every sum, and sums of money due from us respectively, for any *Medicine* or *Medical Attendance,* and for any *Subscription* to any *Sick or Accident Funds* of which we are members, or in the benefits of which we participate, *Fuel* or any *Materials, Tools, or Implements* employed by each of us in our respective trades or occupations, and also for any *Rent* of the whole or any part of a *Tenement* which may be demised to us respectively by the said Company, or occupied by us respectively; and we agree and contract with the said Company that the said Company shall be entitled to make, from our respective wages, every stoppage and deduction which the said Company are by law entitled to make from and out of the wages of any artificer, under the provision of Section 23 of the Act 1 and 2 William IV. ch. 37,

---

*Truck Acts 1831, 1887, and 1896 (1 and 2 William IV. c. 37; 50 and 51 Vict. c. 46; and 59 and 60 Vict. c. 44).

or under any other Act of Parliament, and which are by any such Act required to be authorised in writing.

As Witness our hands.

Date.	Workmen's Names.	*Coal No.	Occupation.	Address.	† Doctor.	Witness.

In addition to this agreement, or combined with it, there is often another agreement which sets out the conditions under which men are to work at the mine in question. At a colliery in Lancashire‡ the useful plan is followed of giving each man, on being engaged, a printed book containing—(1) Abstract of the Coal Mines Regulation Act, (2) Special Rules, and (3) Conditions of Service between the Company and their workmen. The last mentioned rules are very much to the point and are herewith given in full :—

CONDITIONS OF SERVICE

BETWEEN THE..................COAL COMPANY, LIMITED, AND THE COLLIERS AND OTHER WORKMEN EMPLOYED AT THE WORKS OF THE SAID COMPANY AT THE.................. COLLIERY,....................

Being Supplemental to the General and Special Rules, under the Coal Mines Regulation Act, 1887.

1. Every collier to be at the pit, with his lamp or candles (whichever he may use there) and tools in an efficient state, at the proper time in the morning. He will not be allowed to go down before six o'clock, nor to ascend before two o'clock in the afternoon, without the consent of the underlooker or officer in charge, or except in case of accident or sickness.
2. Every collier shall, unless otherwise required, work ten fair days in each fortnight ; and every fireman, furnaceman, and other workman twelve days, if so required, unless prevented by sickness or accident.
3. Where lines are suspended from the roof to show the course of any level, end, or drift, every collier shall work according to such lines, and shall not be paid for so much of his work as shall be out of the course indicated.
4. Every collier shall send his cannel or coal free from dirt. He shall send every tub of coal and slack full, and marked in the usual way by cuts or tallies, and shall not be paid for any tub dirty or without mark.
5. Every workman occupying a house under the company shall be held to have specially agreed that the wages remaining unpaid to such workman at the time of his ceasing to be employed shall not be payable to him until he shall have given up possession of such house and premises.
6. Every collier, dataller§, engineer, banksman, hooker-on, fireman, furnaceman, carpenter, blacksmith, and other workman, shall give fourteen days' notice, in writing, to expire on the day to which wages are made up, before leaving the said Company's employment, and shall receive the same notice before being discharged, except in case of having violated any of these rules or of the general or special rules established at the colliery.
7. Every collier or workman shall, after receiving his earnings, pay to the agents of the said Company, as and for such collier's or workman's contribution to the Miners' Accident Society, established on the works, eightpence per fortnight for himself and eightpence for each drawer employed by him. The society shall be conducted by a committee

---

* The number by which the colliers are afterwards known, and by which they distinguish the waggons of coal they send up.
† The men may choose their own doctor.
‡ I owe various forms from Lancashire to the kindness of Mr. William Kellett, J.P.
§ Workman paid by the day.

consisting of the underlookers employed at the colliery, and an equal number of colliers or other workmen appointed by the men, to which committee shall be handed over the money so paid, and who shall have the sole distribution thereof. All fines for breach of rule shall be handed to the committee, to be added to the funds of the society.

8. No wages shall be paid except on the usual weekly pay-day, and every collier and other workman to whom, at his request, the agents of the said company shall have supplied materials, tools, implements, or other goods for such collier, shall pay for the same the first time after such supply on which he receives his wages, and a like payment shall be made for rent, where any such shall be owing for a dwelling occupied by him under the Company.

9. Every collier in pillar workings where the roof is dangerous and likely to fall shall, without delay, remove into a safe place all tools, props, rails, sleepers, and other materials, the property of the said Company (for doing which he shall be paid), and shall not leave the pit until he has done so, or warned the underlooker or fireman of the dangerous state of his place. In default he shall make good the damage out of wages then due or thereafter to become due to him from the Company.

10. If any collier refuses to prop and to make his place safe, the fireman or officer in charge shall either send such person out of the pit or provide other men to make his place safe, and recover the cost thereof from the person so neglecting to make his place safe. If a place cannot be made safe at once the work must stop until it shall have been made safe.

11. Every drawer not using proper scotches will be sent out of the pit or fined. If fined, the amount will be recoverable from the collier who employs him.

12. No person shall ride up or down any pit whilst the water tanks are attached.

13. Any workman being found on or about the colliery in a state of intoxication, or leaving his work for the purpose of obtaining intoxicating drink, shall be liable to instant dismissal, and fined 5s.; and no workman shall strike or ill-use another, or create any disturbance in the mine, or upon the surface, or use abusive language towards, or interfere with, any officer in the discharge of his duties.

14. Any person smoking during working hours shall be liable to a fine of 1s. for each offence.

15. Any workman absenting himself during working hours without permission shall forfeit any wages he may have earned during that day.

16. For the greater safety of the works and workmen every collier shall, in hiring his drawer, bind the drawer to observe the foregoing rules. The collier shall deliver to the drawer, at the time of such hiring, a printed copy of the rules, to be supplied to him for that purpose by the agents of the said Company. The drawer shall thenceforth, during his employment under such collier at these works, remain subject to these rules. Every collier, so hiring a drawer, shall irrevocably authorise the agents of the Company, in the name of the collier, but at the expense of the Company, to prefer and prosecute any complaint against such drawer for the violation of the rules.

17. Any engineer, when unable to attend his work, shall cause the surface manager to be informed in sufficient time to enable him to find a substitute; and every engineman shall, within one hour after the expiration of his shift, cause the manager or the person in charge of the machinery to be informed of the non-attendance of the engineman who should have relieved him.

18. Every collier or workman, on leaving the Company's employment, shall deliver up to the underlooker his copy of rules, or forfeit the sum of two shillings and sixpence, to be deducted from the wages then due to him.

Having received the pamphlet, the workman signs a book which is ruled thus :—

Name.	Age.	Residence.	Occupation.	Date of engagement.	Date of leaving.	Signature of person employed undertaking to comply with all rules.	Witness.

Sometimes the agreement signed sets forth the conditions and rate of payment. In the Northern Coalfield of England it was customary in times past for colliers to hire themselves by the year. Now fortnightly hiring agreements are in vogue.*

Should a sliding scale (see p. 20) be in use at a mine, it is signed by each workman affected, as well as by representatives of the owners.

It not infrequently happens that miners are sent abroad by Mining Companies whose headquarters are in England. In such cases the terms of the agreement between the miner and the Company are set out in detail, and the agreement is stamped. The following example is illustrative :—

No...........

ARTICLES OF AGREEMENT entered into this..................day of....................One thousand eight hundred and ninety...............between...
................at present residing at.........................in the County of.........................
hereinafter called "the Employé," of the one part, and the... ....
of......................., hereinafter called "the Company," of the other part : WHEREBY each of the said parties hereto agrees with the other of them as follows :—

1. The Employé engages himself as......................................in the service of the said Company for a period of............years, on the following terms and conditions :—
2. The Employé shall proceed to........................, in the State of......................, Mexico, at such time and in such manner as shall be required by the Company.
3. On the arrival of the Employé at..................he shall report himself to the Agent, acting Agent, or other principal officer of the Company for the time being, hereinafter called "the Agent."
4. The Employé shall devote the whole of his time to the service of the Company, and shall faithfully and diligently devote himself to its service in the capacity for which he is engaged, or otherwise as may be directed by the Agent from time to time, so as to make himself useful to the Company.
5. The Employé shall be subservient to, and obey the orders of the said Agent, and shall submit and agree to such arrangements, rules, fines, and penalties as may be imposed by him, and to such working hours per day, and times of working as the said Agent may from time to time direct ; and in like manner obey the orders of his superior officer for the time being under the said Agent.
6. The Employé shall reside in such place, and remove from time to time to such place or places as may be required by the Agent, and he shall not sleep or remain the night away from his station without the authority of the Agent.
7. The Employé shall at all times conduct himself in an orderly and peaceable manner, and above all be sober, and strictly temperate in the use of ardent spirits or other intoxicants, and any breach of this condition shall be deemed misconduct of so grave a character as to justify the Employé's immediate discharge.
8. The Employé shall pay becoming respect to the civil and religious institutions and customs of Mexico, and he shall carefully abstain from interference of any kind with the politics or government of the Country, so as not to give cause of offence in relation thereto.
9. The period of service is to count from the date of the Employé's reporting his arrival to the resident Agent at......................, provided, nevertheless, that any absence occasioned by sickness is to be made up at what would otherwise be the date of the expiration of the Agreement, so that the full term of............years be worked.
10. The Company will, at its own expense, pay the Employé's passage money to ...., and at the expiration of this Agreement a similar return passage to England, if he shall have completed his Agreement to the satisfaction of the Agent, and provided that he return home and report himself at the Office of the Company for the time being, within a period of two months.
11. The Company will allow the Employé half-pay from the date of leaving England, until his arrival at the mines.
12. For the outward journey only the Company will allow such reasonable charges, if any, as the Employé may incur in travelling from his home to the port of departure of the steamer he is directed to proceed by.
13. From the wages as paid to the Employé in...............there shall be deducted ten per cent. as security for the due fulfilment of this contract on his part until it amounts to

---

*For examples, see Bulman and Redmayne, *Colliery Working and Management*, London, 1896, pp. 33, 284, *et seq.*

twenty-five pounds sterling. This security shall be available to pay such amounts as the Agent may in his discretion impose by way of penalty or fine for intemperance, insubordination, malingering, or other misconduct; if such security be at any time or times reduced below the full amount, the said deduction shall recommence until the full amount is again attained. Should the misconduct of the Employé be of such a nature as to warrant his dismissal, and of which the Agent shall be the sole judge, he will be required to return to England, and his return passage will be paid out of the said security so far as it will go, the balance due to him, if any, being paid to him on his reporting himself at the Company's Office in London. The Agent's statement as to any deductions therefrom by way of fines or penalties shall be accepted by both parties as final. In the event of the Employé completing the Agreement in a manner satisfactory to the Agent, the security will be paid to him in full, but no interest will be allowed.

14. Should the Employé be absent from duty by reason of sickness or accident, he will be allowed half-pay during a certain time, to be fixed in each case in the discretion of the Agent, but if the Agent shall be satisfied that such absence was attributable to the Employé's misconduct he shall receive no pay.

15. In the event of the Employé being rendered incapable of performing his duty from ill-health, or by accident, or otherwise, causing permanent or lasting disablement or unfitness for work, of which the Agent, acting on medical advice, shall be the sole judge, this Agreement shall be determined and cease. If such incapacity was not attributable to intemperance or any other imprudence or misconduct on his part, or to any disease contracted previous to this Agreement, the Company will allow and pay the Employé one month's wages, reckoning from the date of his ceasing to work, in addition to his return passage.

16. In the event of the breach, non-observance, or non-performance by the Employé of any of the conditions of this Agreement, then and in such case, the Company or its Agent in Mexico may put an end to and determine this Agreement, and the engagement of the Employé thereunder at once and without notice. And the Employé shall not in this event be entitled to any salary in lieu of notice, nor to a return passage, and he shall forfeit all right, benefit, and advantage reserved to him by this Agreement.

17. This Agreement to be for a period of.........years, dating from the time of the arrival of the Employé at..............., with the option on the part of the Company of retaining his services at the same rate of wages for another year on the expiration of the said term of ....years.

18. In consideration of the Employé duly and faithfully performing his part of this Agreement, the Company shall pay to him during the continuation thereof by way of wages or remuneration, commencing from the date of his reporting himself at..................., and in currency of the country, the sum of.........................pounds sterling per calendar month. A portion of this amount, £.............per month, "Home Pay," dating from arrival at ...., to be paid to...........

19. This Agreement shall have the same effect in Mexico as respects to the laws of Mexico as if the same had been made and concluded in that country, and the Employé agrees to execute a copy of it in Mexico whenever required to do so by the Agent, in such form as is required by, or is conformable to, the laws of that country, and containing the same provisions as are contained in this Agreement.

IN WITNESS whereof....................................and ....two of the Directors, and..........................the Secretary, of the.., have on behalf of the Company, hereunto set their hands, and the said............................ has hereunto set his hand the day and year first above written.

Witness to the Signatures of
....
and......................................
two of the Directors, and..........
........................the Secretary,
of the..................................
....

On behalf of the............................
....
.... } Directors.
....Secretary.

Witness to the Signature of
....

At a mine on the Rand,* the usage is for each European workman to

---

* Mr. J. Harry Johns has kindly supplied me with much valuable information and many forms from the Witwatersrand Goldfield.

ENGAGEMENT OF WORKMEN. 9

sign an agreement with the Company, freeing the Company from any liability whatsoever in case of accident, on the understanding that the Company provides each workman with free insurance against accident.* Each workman also agrees to accept or give a day's notice upon the termination of employment. At the mines of the De Beers Company,† Europeans are engaged by the heads of departments, but particulars must be furnished to the General Manager for his sanction. The following form is used :—

DE BEERS CONSOLIDATED MINES, LTD.

No.

Counterfoil. MEMORANDUM OF NEW EMPLOYÉS.

Date taken on.	Full Christian and Surname.	Trade, or how Employed.	Remarks.

.................................189 ....

NOTE.—*All new employés should be asked if they have ever been in the service of the Company; if so, reason of their leaving must be stated in Remarks column. This form must be sent to the General Manager's Department on the date the employés are engaged.*

Particulars of men leaving or discharged must also be supplied to the General Manager in the next form, which is printed on pink paper to avoid confusion with the last.

DE BEERS CONSOLIDATED MINES, LTD.

No.

Counterfoil. MEMORANDUM OF EMPLOYÉS LEFT OR DISCHARGED.

Date Left or Discharged.	Full Christian and Surname.	Trade, or how Employed.	Reason for Leaving or being Discharged.

.................................189 ....

NOTE.—*This form must be sent to the General Manager's Department on the date the employés leave.*

Finally, every fortnight, before the books are made up for pay-day, the following return must be made to the Paymaster :—

* Owing to the Employers' Liability Act, it is a not uncommon policy in England to insure against accidents to workpeople.
† I am indebted to Mr. Gardner F. Williams, general manager, and to the late Mr. W. H. Craven for forms from De Beers Consolidated Mines.

MINE ACCOUNTS.

DE BEERS CONSOLIDATED MINES, Ltd.

Return of changes in Employés, &c., at............for Fortnight ended.........189

Name.	Occupation.	Date taken on.	Rate of Pay.	Date Discharged or Left.	Change in Rate of Pay.		Remarks.
					From	To	

(Signature)...

NOTE.—*Transfers to be noted in the "Remarks" column thus:—Transferred to .... (opposite name, stating Department).*
Reason why men are discharged or have left to be given in "Remarks" column.
This form to be sent to the Paymaster not later than 2 p.m. on the last day of the pay.
Should there be no change during the fortnight, the sheet to be so marked and sent in as usual.

The above sheet must be initialled by the General Manager, in sign of approval, before it is used by the Paymaster.

Natives can only be engaged with the help of a Government official (*Registrar*), who records the terms agreed on, and gives a contract-note to the employer and a simple form of ticket to the native. The ticket bears a shilling stamp.

At a colliery in Spain, two forms are in use; they are bound up in two books with counterfoils; one, which remains with the under-agents, is for suggesting that a certain workman be employed; the other, kept by the General Manager, authorises the employment of the workman.*

Both the Coal† and Metalliferous Mines Regulation‡ Acts regulate the employment of boys, girls, and women about mines, and provide further that a register of such must be kept. Official forms are prescribed.

The surface works of mines under the Metalliferous Act, such as dressing works and repairing shops, and all quarries, come within the jurisdiction of the Factory and Workshop Acts of 1878,§ 1891,|| and 1895.¶ The surface works of mines under the Coal Mines Act are not affected by these Acts, and even in the case of brickworks attached to collieries, it is only when bricks are made for sale that the works are subject to the statutes relating to factories.

These Acts regulate the employment of children, young persons and women, and the Act of 1878 provides that there shall be kept "in the prescribed form and with the prescribed particulars, registers of the children and young persons employed, and of their employment, and of other matters under this Act."** The prescribed form of register is to be obtained from the official publishers at 3d. per copy.

If a list of workpeople, with date of first employment and other particulars, is not obtained by making them sign an agreement, it is advisable to have such a list made specially, with a column for date of leaving, as it forms a permanent record, and is frequently useful for reference. The following form is an example:—

* Oriol, *Contabilidad Minera*. Madrid, 1894, p. 45.
† Coal Mines Regulation Act, 1887 (50 and 51 Vict. ch. 58), sec. 4, 5, 6, 7, and 8.
‡ Metalliferous Mines Regulation Act, 1872 (35 and 36 Vict. ch. 77), sec. 4, 5, and 6.
§ 41 and 42 Vict. ch. 16. || 54 and 55 Vict. ch. 75.
¶ 58 and 59 Vict. ch. 37. ** Sec. 77.

Date when engaged.	Name.	Age.	Residence.	Occupation.	Date of leaving.

Period between Pay-days.—Colliers are often paid every week. This is a very short interval between pay-days, and it causes a weekly recurring strain on the officials in collecting the necessary information, and on the clerks in making up the pay-books; still, it is a system in considerable favour with the men. Generally three days' or a week's pay is kept in hand; that is to say, a collier paid on a Saturday would only receive the money due to him up to the previous Wednesday, or Saturday, the intervening days being necessary for the calculation of the amounts due, and for making up the pay-books.

A modification of the weekly pay system is that in which the amounts due on contracts are only made up once a fortnight; on alternate weeks, the men working on contract receive a certain sum on account, called "subsist."

Fortnightly "pays" are fairly common, especially in metalliferous mines; they relieve the staff, and seem to answer very well for all concerned. Generally a week's pay is kept in hand, but there are exceptions to this; thus, at Carn Brea Mine in Cornwall, a week's pay is kept in hand for those workmen paid by the day, while for contract-men a fortnight's pay is kept in hand.

Monthly* "pays" are still met with in the Isle of Man, Colorado, Spain, and other countries; but the period is somewhat long. The old style in Cornwall was to have monthly "pays," and to keep a month's pay in hand; so that it was possible for a man to work more than seven weeks before receiving any money. This was a great hardship; hence the interval between "pays" and amount to be kept in hand are now regulated by the Stannaries Act, 1887,† by which payment must be made fortnightly, and not more than seven days' pay must be kept in hand for surfacemen, or fourteen days' pay for contract-men. The contracts made often run for two months, in which case the miner receives "subsist" at intermediate "pays," the balance due to him on his contract being handed over on the pay-day next after the two months are ended.

On the Rand, monthly "pays" are in vogue, Europeans being paid every calendar month, as soon after the end of the month as the accounts can be completed, and natives every four weeks. There is, however, a native pay-day every week, as the "boys" do not all complete their four weeks at the same time.

CHAPTER II.—DATA DETERMINING GROSS AMOUNT DUE TO WORKMEN.

THE gross amount of money due to workmen may be determined by—

    A. Length of time worked,
    B. Amount of work done,
    C. Value of mineral gotten,

or by a combination of these factors.

* Generally twenty-eight days, though sometimes a calendar month.
† 50 and 51 Vict. ch. 43, sec. 11.

A. LENGTH OF TIME WORKED.

Most of the men working *at the surface* of mines are paid by the day—*e g.*, foremen, clerks, storekeepers, carpenters, mechanics, masons, engine-drivers, platelayers, pit-top hands (banksmen), millmen, and labourers. In addition, certain classes of *underground* workmen are also paid by the day—*e.g.*, haulage attendants, onsetters, platelayers, &c.; but in Britain the system of paying by the day is not usual for the actual mineral-getters, whose wages are generally reckoned by amount of work done, or by the value of the mineral obtained. In South Africa, Colorado, and many other countries, however, miners and trammers are not infrequently paid a day wage.

A careful record of the length of time worked by all the men in this class is kept by an official appointed for the purpose, who may also act as foreman, or, in small concerns, as storekeeper. Sometimes the workmen are required to present themselves at the timekeeper's office, to take out a ticket or a check, when they commence work in the morning, as is usual in large engineering shops and factories; but this is not general. If the number of men is not very large, the timekeeper, as a rule, satisfies himself of their presence or absence by visiting them at their work, and making a record in a pocket time-book. The following is an example :—

TIME WORKED AT...................MINES, FORTNIGHT ENDING...................18......

Name.	Employment.	S.	M.	T.	W.	T.	F.	S.	S.	M.	T.	W.	T.	F.	S.	Total.
John Jones,	Labourer,	...	1	1	¾	1	1	1	...	¾	1	1	1	1	1	11¼

The pencilled entries in this rough Time-book are transferred by the time-keeper to a larger Time-book kept in the office, which is ruled similarly, but with two additional columns, one for the rate per day, and the other for the amount of money due. From this latter book the information is extracted for the pay-sheets.

Sometimes only one book is used; in this case it is provided with a column for rate per day or hour, and a column for amount of money due. The period provided for in each opening depends upon the interval between pay-days.

Less than a quarter of a day is not generally noted; a stroke indicates a full day, fractions being marked in quarters, as shown in the above example. Another plan is to make a square represent a full day; each side then stands for a quarter of a day. This method has the advantage of showing which quarter or half day a workman has missed. Thus, suppose he missed a quarter in the morning, his mark would be ⊓, whereas if he went away early in the afternoon it would be ⊔; the square being, as it were, built up during the day, always in the same order.

At a gold mine in South Africa the time of the natives is kept by the overseers and timekeeper in the usual way; but in addition, each native receives a ticket, which is initialled by the timekeeper for each day worked. Provision is made on it for twenty-eight days, and, when full, it is exchanged for a pay ticket, if it agrees with the timekeeper's and overseer's Time-books. Each native working overtime receives a special ticket, which is white for a full shift, and pink for half a shift :—

GROSS AMOUNT DUE TO WORKMEN.

PAY TICKET.

..................GOLD MINING Co. (LIMITED).
No.............
Name,............................
Due, Date,........................
Amount, £   :   :
Place where Working,............
....
....

OVERTIME TICKET.
.....................G. M. Co., LD.
Kaffir Overtime.

By Thursday morning all Kaffir pay tickets, issued for the week ending on the Wednesday evening previous, are entered in the Kaffir pay-book, and the amount of money required for the native pay can be determined.*

In Time-books the names of the men are classified according to the kind of work upon which they are employed. Thus the carpenters, mechanics, masons and engine-drivers would be kept together; while the labourers, in the case of a colliery for instance, employed in screening and picking, washing, coking, and briquette-making, would all be classified under these heads. The chief reason for this grouping is the facility it offers for making an analysis of the cost of each department, and for comparing the wages paid to men doing a similar class of work.

In addition to the time recorded by the Timekeeper, skilled workmen, such as fitters, carpenters, smiths, and masons, keep time-sheets on which each man records daily the work at which he has been employed, and the number of hours he has worked at each job. These time-sheets are signed by the foreman. They are useful as a check on the men, for calculating the cost of any new work, and for distributing the cost of repairs among the different departments.

The following is a simple example of a time-sheet :—

....................CO.—.....................MINES.

Week ending....................................1895.

....................................'s TIME-SHEET.

	Working for	What doing	Hours.	Total.
SUNDAY.				
MONDAY.				

Overtime.—Overtime is sometimes recorded in a separate book, and sometimes in the ordinary Time-book by using red ink, or in some other dis-

* See also Hatch & Chalmers, *Gold Mines of the Rand*, London, 1895, page 267; and Salisbury, "Mining Accounts," *Trans. Incorporated Accountants' Students' Society of London*, 1894, p. 71.

tinctive manner. Employers, however, very generally object to overtime, as it is natural to suppose that if a man is going to work three or four hours overtime, he will not put his best energies into his ordinary day's work; further, it is easier for a workman to make a job last out, if by so doing he can get a few shillings extra, than it is to detect such frauds. Certain work about a mine, such as repairs to engines, must necessarily be done out of ordinary working hours; but this is often arranged for by making the men take an equal amount of time out of their ordinary day.

Save in certain exceptional cases, young persons are prevented by the Factory Acts from working overtime at the surface works of mines under the Metalliferous Act, or at quarries; if any overtime is worked, a register must be kept and notice sent to the Inspector of Factories * for the district. The official book consists of notices to be sent to the Inspector, with counterfoils which remain in the workshop.

The Acts also provide that a minimum number of holidays in the year must be given to children, young persons, and women, and these must be recorded in the prescribed register mentioned on p. 10.

B. AMOUNT OF WORK DONE.

This is almost invariably the factor which determines the gross amount of money due to miners in Britain; and, not infrequently, certain kinds of surface work also are paid for in this way. In Cornwall, the work paid for in this manner is called "tutwork;" in other districts, "piece work," or "contract work," or "bargain work." It has the advantage that it enables a good workman to obtain some benefit from his greater skill, or the greater energy he may display; and, where it is possible to make the interests of the miner and his employer identical, it is also to the benefit of the latter.

Sinking and Driving.—In sinking shafts and driving levels, payment is made according to linear measurement, the shaft or level being maintained of the dimensions agreed on. In many metalliferous mines in England, the unit is the fathom; in collieries, the yard; in South Africa, Colorado, and other places where labour is dear, the foot; and on the Continent, the metre. It is generally part of the agreement that the verticality, or the inclination of the shaft, or the direction of the level, is to be strictly maintained according to instructions.

This class of work is known as "dead-work," because it is not directly profitable, although it is a necessary preliminary to the profitable working of a mine. The German phrase for dead-work, *Todtwerk*, introduced into this country by the German miners brought over by Queen Elizabeth, has given rise to the term "tutwork" mentioned above, which has, however, acquired a more extended meaning.

The necessary measuring is done generally by the underground manager, but sometimes by the mine-surveyor, as in Colorado. Permanent marks, conveniently near the end of the drift or heading, or bottom of the shaft, are made or noted from time to time as starting points for the measurements. The distances are usually recorded in an ordinary memorandum book; but it is better to use a book specially ruled, and kept exclusively for this work. Such a book is a great help to accuracy, and is useful for future reference. Here is an example:—

* Inspectors of Mines are Inspectors of Factories and Workshops for their districts, as far as mines and quarries more than 20 feet deep, are concerned.

GROSS AMOUNT DUE TO WORKMEN. 15

Name of Company.	*Gross Measurement.			†Deduct Mark.			Net Measurement.			Price per Fm.		‡New Mark.	
	Fm.	Ft.	In.	Fm.	Ft.	In.	Fm.	Ft.	In.	£	s.	Fm.	Ft.	In.

Another column could very usefully be added to this form for containing a memorandum of the distance of the end from the commencement of a drift or heading; this should be checked from time to time by actual measurement, and also by comparing the length with that shown by the plan. These precautions are necessary, as there is no doubt that frequently a greater length is paid for than is actually driven.

Generally only one measurement is made between pay-days—viz., on a day as near the following pay-day as can be conveniently arranged; but at a mine in South Africa, where monthly "pays" are in vogue, measurements are taken every Monday morning, in addition to the monthly measurements. These are all recorded in a measuring book, as under :—

MEASURING BOOK.

Date.	Working Place.	Reef.	Weekly Advance.		Total Advance.		From	Width of Reef.	Remarks.
			Ft.	Ins.	Ft.	Ins.			

Exploitation.—When a mineral deposit is being worked away, payment may be made according to :—

    a. Volume excavated.
    b. Weight of mineral gotten.
    c. Volume of mineral gotten.
    d. Depth of holes bored.

a. Volume Excavated.—In vein-mining the price paid is often so much per *square* fathom, measured in the plane of the lode, the whole width of the lode being taken away; in the case either of a very wide lode or of a mass deposit, the price may be reckoned per *cubic* fathom. Where no selection of the ore is required, and everything broken has to be sent to the surface, this method is fairly satisfactory; but where the ore has to be sorted underground, it is not at all applicable, because the miners are solely interested in making as large a hole as possible before the measuring-day, whereas the proprietors are interested in the amount and quality of the ore sent to the surface. Under these circumstances the miners sometimes throw away "stuff" they have broken on to the "stulls," and into old workings, instead of taking the trouble to pick out the good ore and send it to the shaft. This difficulty is got over to some extent by giving a premium on ore sent to the surface in addition to the price per cubic fathom; however, the interest of the miner and proprietor can only be made identical by giving the former a proportion of the value of the ore when it is ready for the market. When the vein is irregular in richness (as is often the case with copper, tin, lead, and zinc lodes), the value of the ore obtained does

    * Distance of end or face from last mark.
    † Distance of end or face from last mark on previous measuring day.
    ‡ Distance of new mark from the face.

not necessarily bear any relation to the amount of vein broken—that is, to the amount of work done—and so the method of payment applicable to such cases comes under the next head (C).

Where mineral is being excavated in an open quarry and requires no selection, payment by volume excavated is suitable. The cubic yard is, in such cases, the common unit.

b. Weight of Mineral Gotten.—This is almost invariably the method used in working coal; and it is likewise common in working stratified ironstone, hæmatite, and many other minerals. The "bargains" are generally arranged at so much per ton of mineral weighed at the surface.

At collieries a weighing-machine is provided close to the pit-top, on which each waggon-load of coal is weighed as soon as it reaches the surface. The Coal Mines Regulation Act provides that a check-weigher may be stationed at the pit-top, to look after the interests of the men, if the majority of them so elect; and this is the general practice.

The man, or company of men, to whom a particular waggon-load "belongs," is indicated by a tin or leathern tally fastened to it, and bearing a number; or, a number is chalked on the side of the waggon. This number may be the number of the stall where the man is working, or it may be a number given to the man when engaged, and which he retains as long as he remains at that colliery. The weights of coal are recorded on a sheet, or in a book, under these numbers. Generally the sheet is of considerable size, so that a single one takes the whole output for the day; or in the case of a book two opposite pages are made to suffice in order to avoid turning over the leaves. Here is a simple example, which can, of course, be greatly extended :—

OUTPUT AT................PIT.................189...

1	2	3	4	5	6	7	8	9	10	11	12	13	14	T.	C.	Q.

The daily total for each number is got by vertical addition, while the horizontal addition of these totals gives the total for the day. The same result is obtained by vertically adding the totals got by the horizontal addition of each line; by computing both ways a check is obtained.

From these daily records a weekly summary is made for the purposes of the pay-sheets, as shown below :—

No.	Monday.	Tuesday.	Wednesday.	Thursday.	Friday.	Saturday.	Totals	Croppings.	Net Total.

The "croppings" are deductions for shale sent out with the coal. If a waggon contains much refuse, the foreman at the screens has the shale in it set aside; this he shows to the check-weigher or to the collier himself, and a deduction is made equal to perhaps twice the weight of the shale picked out, as a sort of fine. The foreman in the above case keeps a record of these deductions, but sometimes—indeed most frequently—no separate record is kept, the amounts being knocked off at once from the weights of the waggon-loads in question. In some collieries the whole weight of the load is struck out.

In working steam coal in South Wales, only the round coal is paid for. The total weight of the coal in the waggon is first ascertained; then the coal is tipped on to a screen with bars some 1¼ in. apart; the small falls through into a box, and its weight is indicated on the face of a dial and recorded. Thus two records are kept, one of all the coal, the other of the small; it is only at the end of the week that the total of the latter is subtracted from that of the former.

In the case of hæmatite, the ore is occasionally weighed at the pit-top; more generally, however, it is not weighed until loaded into railway waggons; an account is kept of the number of small pit waggon-loads, and at the end of the week the total weight is apportioned between them. The Metalliferous Mines Regulation Act of 1872 makes no provision for the appointment of a check-weigher.

In Cornwall, when tutwork men are paid according to the number of tons of tinstone raised, the weight is generally ascertained by simply counting the number of waggons; the average weight carried by a waggon being known approximately. This is really payment according to volume. The Stannaries Act, 1887, provides that the miners may appoint a check-weigher if they wish; but practically this is never done.

Notched pegs are sometimes used for identifying waggons instead of numbers. The first records are often kept in a primitive manner, by chalking marks on a board, or by pegging small holes in a lump of clay.

c. *Volume of Mineral Gotten.*—It was pointed out above that sometimes the payment, although ostensibly according to weight, is really made according to volume. The following are other examples of the same kind:—
At the De Beers mines, excavation of diamond-bearing rock (*blue ground*) is paid for per load of 16 cubic feet; and at Rio Tinto* the mineral is excavated by the ton, the number of tons being ascertained by multiplying the number of trucks by the approximate weight in each.

The example on this page shows the method of booking. This is adapted to the monthly "pays" there in vogue, and is written up from a book kept by the teller (*contador*), whose business it is to count the trucks.

d. *Depth of Holes Bored.*—This method is employed in stoping the wide lead lodes in the Upper Hartz.† The holes are planned by a foreman, who also measures them when bored and fires them. The price is 1 m. 38 pf. (1s. 4½d.) per metre of hole bored upwards, and 1 m. 13 pf. (1s. 1½d.) per metre of hole bored downwards.

Conveying (*tramming, trailing, putting, drawing*) the valuable mineral or the waste rock to the shaft may be part of the bargain taken by the miner, or it may form a separate bargain. ‡ In the latter case, the data determining the

---

* Mr. James Osborne, M.I.C.E., and Mr. P. B. Waugh, A.R.S.M., have both supplied me with useful information and forms from the Rio Tinto Mines.
† Foster, *Ore and Stone Mining*. London, 1894, p. 639.

money to be paid may be just the same as in the miner's bargain, but the price will, of course, be less. Thus youths will undertake to keep a rock-drift clear at so much per fathom driven; mineral is often trammed at so much per ton; and "blue ground" at Kimberley is trammed at so much per load. At collieries there is sometimes an agreement whereby tramming is paid for according to distance and the inclination of the roads.

Although the main part of the work done by men may be paid for by the fathom, yard, ton, or load, there is often other incidental work for which they are paid separately, but at prices previously agreed on. It may also happen that men are temporarily set to work which has not been mentioned in their agreement; in this case payment is usually reckoned at the current rate for day-work. Further, unforeseen circumstances may arise, through no fault of their own, which prevent them prosecuting their work; thus they may be "drowned out" of a shaft, or out of dip workings, owing to a stoppage of the pumps; and therefore *extras* and *allowances* are often found in workmen's pay accounts. It is very necessary that all these should be seen to by the manager, personally if possible. Generally a simple memorandum book is used to record them, though a suitably ruled form is a great help to clearness; it makes the record more permanently useful, and saves time. When such a book is used, it commonly serves in addition as a measurement book. The following is an example from *Llanbradach Colliery, South Wales:—

Date.	No.	Name.	No. of stall.	No. of men.	Heading.	Double shift in stall.	Airways.	Carting.	Top.	Bottom.	Projs.	Cogs.	Partings.	Turning stalls.	Days.	Allowance.	Remarks.

The details in the above are set out more fully in the *due-bill* on p. 31.

Sometimes no allowances whatever are made, the miners taking their share of the risk of loss by unforeseen hindrances.

In past times "bargain work" was let by public auction in Cornwall,† but nowadays it is generally a matter of private agreement. There is not, however, any signed contract as a rule, the bargain being simply entered in a book, provided for the purpose, by the officials.

Here is an example from Cornwall ‡ of a "tutwork setting book":—

---

* Prof. William Galloway designed most of the forms used at Llanbradach, and I have to thank him for permission to employ them.
† *Mining Journal*, vol. ii. London, 1836, p. 207.
‡ Mr. William Thomas, A.M.I.C.E., gave me much help in collecting information relating to Cornish mine accounts.

GROSS AMOUNT DUE TO WORKMEN.

TUTWORK SETTING.   For 4 weeks ending............189

		£	s.	d.

John Wills and Pare * to drive the 420 fms. level East of Engine Shaft by 15 men. Taken at £25 per fathom By John Wills. (*Here would follow a full list of the names of the other men, if there had been any alteration in the pare since the last bargain was made.*)	John Wills and Pare driving the 420 fms. level East of the Engine Shaft by 15 men.
	
	 fms. ft. ins.
	 Measured 12 4 6
	 Mark 5 3 0
	           ───────
	           7 1 6 at £25 per fm.
	 Sundry repairs to pitwork, two months, .
		181
		
		37
			5
			
			2
				0
				
				0

£25 per fathom for 10 fathoms. To pay for drawing (*winding the mineral up the shaft*).		218	7	0
(Left-hand page).	(Right-hand page).			

In this case the terms of the bargain are written on the left-hand page, and the gross money due on the right-hand page. It will be noticed that the "bargain" is to run, not for a definite time, but until a definite length of level has been driven.

The following is an example of a "setting book" from the Rand :—

MINE CONTRACT BOOK.

Date of setting.	Name of Contractor.	Position of working place.	Conditions of Contract.	Setting price.			Per	Percentage to be deducted.	Payments to be made.	Remarks.
				£	s.	d.				

Occasionally a written agreement setting forth in full the various conditions of the contract is employed. Or the conditions under which the work has to be done may be posted on the mine, and the men asked to tender prices.

The following short example † from Kimberley will illustrate the latter method :—

..................................MINE,

..................................189

To CONTRACTORS.

Tenders are invited, and will be received by the undersigned up to 12 o'clock, Saturday, ____, 189 ___, at the Mine Office.

For sinking the main shaft below the ____ ft. level. Inside dimensions of the shaft to be 20 ft. 6 in. × 6 ft. Timber sets to be 6 ft. apart ; and hitches, for end bearers, to be cut 6 in. deep every sixth set. The shaft to be well squared on the sides and ends, to be sunk plumb ; and the timber well and truly set.

The contractors to find all labour, tools, stores, and explosives. The Company finding enginemen and rock drills, and keeping the latter in repair. When the shaft is cut out to its full size, four rock drills may be employed. Five per cent. of amounts due each pay-day will be retained until the sinking of the length tendered for has been completed. The whole of the work to be done to the satisfaction of the General Manager.

.... *Mine Manager.*

---

* A "pare" is a company of men associated together in a bargain.
† For other examples, see Bulman and Redmayne, *op. cit.*, pp. 89, 90, 292, *et seq.*

Sliding-Scales.—In the case of coal and stratified ironstone, the prices for getting mineral are frequently more uniform than is possible in other kinds of mining, and sliding-scales have been used to a considerable extent to determine the average wages. They are based upon the selling price of coal or iron, as the case may be; a certain standard price corresponding to a certain standard wage. If prices go up, wages go up in a proportion fixed by the sliding-scale, and *vice versâ*. The selling prices are determined by accountants sworn to secrecy.

Various examples of sliding-scale agreements have been given by Professor Munro in two papers, one read before the British Association in 1885* and the other before the Manchester Statistical Society in 1889.† Of late, however, sliding-scales have been less in favour among coal miners than they used to be.

There is one instance of a sliding-scale in hæmatite mines. It is based upon the price of pig iron.

Sometimes it is extremely difficult to get men who have been used to day wage to work upon contract. They are afraid of the risk, as it naturally takes a little time for prices to become equitably adjusted. This difficulty was met at a small gold mine in New South Wales in the following manner:—The average daily output of ore for the last twelve months was taken as a basis; from this and the wages received by the various workmen concerned with the getting or treatment of the ore, a price per ton was calculated. For instance, it was found that 36 miners at 7s. 6d. per day each, had raised on an average 55 tons of gold quartz per day. A ton of quartz had therefore cost 4s. 11d., and this price was agreed upon as a standard. If more than 55 tons were raised per day, which one can imagine was quite possible, it would mean that the miners would receive higher wages. The price per ton to be paid to the other workmen was calculated in a similar manner. In addition, should the quartz yield above 10 dwts. of gold per ton, a bonus on the prices calculated as above, of 5 per cent. for each dwt. over 10 dwt. of free gold per ton was to be paid. This may serve as an example of a sliding-scale in gold mining.

Though much surface work is paid for by the day, as already explained, yet contracts are not infrequent; for instance, the landing, screening, and picking of coal is often done at so much per ton; for though the amount of coal treated cannot be varied by those at the surface, fewer hands will be required if each individual works harder.

Again, when such excavating has to be done as making drains, cutting for a siding, digging a reservoir, &c., where the object is not the getting of valuable mineral, the work is generally let at so much per cubic yard.

It is important that the time of all contract-men should be kept, so that the average wages of each gang can be correctly calculated. These figures are often necessary for settling labour disputes. The useful practice is followed at some collieries of having numbered metal checks on a board near the pit bottom; as the miners go to their work each takes the check bearing his number, so that a glance at the board tells who is underground and who is not; as the men return, they replace their checks on the board.

Where the time worked by the miners is irregular, an ordinary time-book may be used; but when the time worked is regular, it is simpler to keep an account of lost time only, and not one of the time worked.

Modifications.—Premiums or bonuses are often given, in addition to a

---

* *Sliding-Scales in the Coal Industry.* Manchester, 1885.
† *Sliding-Scales in the Coal and Iron Industries from 1885 to 1889.* Manchester, 1890. See also Price, "Sliding-Scales and other methods of wage arrangements in the north of England," *Journal of the Statistical Society of London*, vol. l., p. 5, 1887.

price per yard or per fathom, in order to induce men to work more quickly; such payments are made when more than a certain length has been driven in a fixed time. At the large stone quarries of Quenast in Belgium, premiums are given to encourage the quarry-men to stick to their work regularly, instead of wasting their time in public-houses.*

At a small mine in North Wales, a combination of day-work and piece-work is in vogue.† The miners are chiefly engaged in boring holes with machine drills driven by compressed air. They receive a fixed wage of a pound a week, and in addition a penny per foot for every foot bored over 12 feet per day of eight hours; they are thus enabled to make three or four shillings a week extra pay, for they can bore 40 or 50 feet a week more than the standard task.

C. VALUE OF MINERAL GOTTEN.

In this method a certain proportion, perhaps the half or even two-thirds, of the value of the mineral broken and prepared for the market determines the gross amount of money due to the miner. Certain deductions are made for materials supplied, and also for winding and dressing the ore; these will be spoken of in the next chapter. This system, known in Cornwall as tributing, is necessarily confined to cases in which valuable mineral can be extracted at once, or in the near future; and even then, when the mineral occurs in large quantities and is of uniform character, as in the case of coal or iron ore, the value of mineral gotten depends on the amount of work done, and the method differs in no wise from those described under the last heading. When the mineral is of greater intrinsic value, however, and occurs in a comparatively narrow vein which varies in richness, then the value of the ore obtained depends partly on the amount of work done, partly on the intelligence and powers of observation of the miner, and to some extent on chance.

This method of payment, therefore, tends to make the miner observant, and to develop his intellectual powers; this is evidently an advantage to him and to the mining company for whom he works. As, moreover, the profits of a rich discovery are shared, in part, by the miner, to whose skill and energy it may be due, it will be seen that this system possesses many advantages. In the early part of the present century it was often spoken of with unqualified praise;‡ but Professor Le Neve Foster has clearly pointed out that it has grave drawbacks;§ the chief of which is that it encourages duplicity, owing to the men being tempted to deceive the manager as to any approaching improvement in their working place (pitch), in order that their contract price may not be reduced. Further, there is a strong temptation to transfer ore by arrangement between two "pares" from a rich "pitch," which will naturally carry a low tribute price, to a poor pitch, where a higher price will rule. The element of gambling, also, which is inherent in the system, is to be deprecated.

Tributing, however, is advantageous in cases where the ore requires careful sorting, for it prevents valuable ore from being left underground, and worthless matrix from being sent to the surface. It is also useful in cleaning out the remnants of a deposit, the main portion of which has already been removed.

In Colorado ‖ the tribute system is met with on an extended scale. A miner, or company of miners, takes a part of a mine to work on lease, instead of a single "pitch" as is usual in Cornwall; in this they are often assisted by outside capital, and even the owners of the mine may take an interest in the venture.

* Foster, *Op. cit.*, p. 652.   † *Idem*, p. 641.
‡ *Journ. of the Statistical Soc. of London*, vol. i., 1838, p. 74.
§ Foster, *Op. cit.*, p. 644, *et seq.*   ‖ Foster, *Op. cit.*, pp. 648 and 649.

In Cornwall, as in the case of tutwork bargains (p. 18), tribute "pitches" used to be let by public auction; but nowadays the contracts are mostly arranged privately between the manager and men, and are recorded in a "Tribute Setting Book."

The gross amount of money due to each gang of men may be ascertained either by dressing as a separate lot all the ore sent by each gang, or by weighing the undressed ore and determining its mineral contents by an assay, after which all the various lots can be mixed together for dressing. The former method necessitates a great number of small operations, which add considerably to the expense of dressing; it is used sometimes in the case of lead and zinc ores.* The latter method is in vogue in Cornwall in dealing with tin ore. A parcel of ore sent to the surface by a company of men is divided into five parts (*doles*), and one of these is weighed and carefully sampled, as representing the rest. The proportion of clean cassiterite is ascertained by washing a definite weight of the sample on a vanning shovel; a simple calculation then gives the amount in the whole parcel of ore sent out. One-eighth is knocked off for loss in dressing. The following is an example of a Sampling-book :—

WHEAL CHANCE TIN SAMPLING FOR...........................18...

Date.	Tributer.	Tinstuff.†			Pro- duce.‡	Black Tin.§			Remarks.
		Tons.	Cwts.	Qrs.		Tons.	Cwts.	Qrs.	Lbs.	
Dec. 19.	John Mundy	10	0	0	2¼	...	2	1	0	
	Wm. Hancock	11	14	0	2¾	...	3	0	6	

CHAPTER III.—DEDUCTIONS.

It has already been mentioned (p. 4) that deductions are made from the gross wages earned by workmen, and that in making them it is necessary to be guided by the provisions of the Truck Acts. Their character varies locally, but as it chiefly depends upon the way in which the men are paid, we will consider them under the three heads adopted in the last chapter.

    A. Where wages are determined by time worked.
    B. Where wages are determined by amount of work done.
    C. Where wages are determined by value of mineral gotten.

A. **Wages Determined by Time Worked.**—Perhaps the most general deductions are those for benefit clubs. Individual mines very frequently have accident or sick clubs, the former paying a weekly allowance in case of accident only, and the latter in case of sickness as well as accident. These clubs are managed by joint committees, composed of representatives elected by the men, and officials of the mining company. There are also district and county clubs which extend their operations over considerable areas.

These clubs often provide other benefits besides the weekly allowance mentioned above, such as an allowance in case of death, medical attendance for the miner and his family, old-age pensions, and regular allowance to the widow

---

* Foster, *Op. cit.*, p. 645.
† Tinstuff = undressed ore.
‡ Produce = parts of cassiterite in 200 of ore (or double the percentage) less one-eighth to allow for loss in dressing.
§ Black tin = dressed tin ore ready for the smelter.

or dependent relative of a miner killed. Contributions are also sometimes made to the funds of local hospitals. Not infrequently the contribution to a sick-club does not include medical attendance, a separate deduction being made for this under the head of "doctor."

Deductions for benefit clubs vary very much in character and amount. Sometimes the deductions are the same for every member; thus at a group of hæmatite mines in Furness, each member pays 6d. per week, and in return, when unable to work on account of sickness or accident, receives 1s. 8d. per day. In Cornwall 6d. to 9d. per member is deducted every month, and in case of accident "hurt pay" to the amount of 1s. per day is paid; there is generally a further deduction for "doctor" of about 1s. per month in the case of a married man, or half that amount in the case of a bachelor.

In other cases the deduction depends more or less upon the wages earned; thus, at De Beers Mine, 6s. per month is deducted if the wages amount to or exceed 11s. per day, and 4s. if wages are less than 11s. In return the miner is insured against death for £100, gets "sick pay," and has the free services of a doctor, while his wife and family are attended at half fees. At a gold mine in Transylvania a percentage is deducted—3 per cent. (3 kreutzer per gulden) for the sick fund, or 5 per cent. for sick fund with pension.

At some mines in Colorado $1 per month is deducted for the hospital, but there is no deduction for benefit clubs, and at many mines even the hospital contribution is not deducted.

At a gold mine in South Africa the natives receive medical attendance and medicines, and are allowed the use of a hospital free. Europeans pay 4s. per month, and this gives them the services of the mine doctor, and medicines.

The accounts of a benefit club must be kept independent of the general accounts of the mining company, so that the financial position of the club can be seen at any time. The total of the deductions, which are obtained from the pay-sheets (described in the next chapter) every pay-day, gives the income. A book, of which the following is an example, is kept to show the details of money paid to members:—

.............................MINES.

Sick Pay for Fortnight ending........................189......

Name.	When taken ill.	Nature of illness.	Resumed work.	No. of weeks on club during current illness.	Payable to	No. of days.	Rate.	Amount.	Deductions.			Total deductions.	Net amount due.	When in receipt of sick pay before.
									Rent.	Club and hospital.	Doctor.			

Each man must produce a doctor's certificate as to unfitness for work, the sick pay counting from the date of the certificate.

Besides this book, all that is necessary is a small ledger, the character of which the student will have no difficulty in understanding after reading Chap. X. In this are entered the totals of income, the totals of payments to members, and any other outgoings, such as funeral expenses and printing expenses; from it are extracted the various items for making a yearly balance-sheet.

Sometimes a mining company has a number of cottages built for the accommodation of its workpeople, in which case there is a deduction for rent. The following example of a Rent Book has a separate column for each fortnightly payment for half-a-year:—

.... MINING COMPANY.
House Rent Roll, *Half year ending* .... 18......

Street and No.	Tenant.	Weekly rent.	Arrears brought forward.	Half-yearly rent.	Total.	Fortnightly payments.			Total amount received.	Empty.	Arrears carried forward.
						Jan.	Feb.	&c.			

At collieries the workmen are generally allowed a certain amount of coal at cost price, this being deducted from their wages. It will be evident that care is necessary to prevent abuse of this privilege. The men can only get the coal at the yard on production of a ticket which they obtain at the office. The following is an example, showing the part which the workman gives to the weigher; there is a counterfoil which remains in the book at the office :—

No............	*No*............
The..................COLLIERY CO., LTD.,	The..................COLLIERY CO., LTD.
.....................COLLIERIES.	.....................COLLIERIES.
Date,.......................189...	Date,.......................189...
To the Weigher,	**WORKMAN'S NOTE FOR HOUSE COAL**
Please supply Bearer :—	(solely for your own household purposes).
Name, ...	Name, ...
Occupation, ...	Occupation, ...
Address, ...	Address, ...
with a load of House Coal solely for his own use. WEIGHT.	WEIGHT.
Gross, ...	Gross, ...
Tare, ...	Tare, ...
Net, ...	Net, ...
Haulier,..	Haulier,..
Weigher, ...	Weigher, ...

Half of this form is returned by the weigher to the workman with the weight of the coal he has received recorded on it; the other half he retains as a record, and as his authorisation for delivering the coal to the workman.

From the part of the ticket so retained the weighman makes up a book, arranged thus :—

.... COLLIERIES.
Account of House-Coal Sold to Workmen.

Date	No. of Note.	Name.	No. on Coal.	Occupation.	Address.	Officials and Landowners.*	Quantity.			Per Ton.	Amount Chargeable.			Charged through Pay Sheet, Week ending
							T.	C.	Q.		£	s.	d.	
							T.	C.	Q.					

* Officials and landowners, in this case, get coal free; but, of course, an account of the amount supplied must be recorded, and it is done in this book.

In Leicestershire a cart-load of coal per month is given free to each workman who is a house-holder.

When men who work by the day are employed underground, they have, in some collieries, to pay for the oil burnt in their lamps. A penny a day is not an unusual charge. In other cases 6d. a week is uniformly charged, for which the mining company supplies oil, cleans the lamps regularly, and keeps them in repair; or, again, there may be no charge either for lamps or oil.

Tools, materials, and stores are generally provided free for this class of workmen by the employer.

B. **Wages Determined by Amount of Work Done.**—The deductions spoken of under the last heading—for benefit club, rent, coal, and oil—are also made in this case, so that what was there said need not be repeated; but, in addition, men working by contract generally pay for tools, candles, and other stores supplied, and also for the sharpening of tools. However, practice varies in this respect very much, sometimes even in the same district.

At a colliery in Cumberland, for instance, each collier has a set of tools given him on starting work, for which he does not pay (except when he loses any by carelessness), neither are stores paid for; but oil is charged 1d. per day, and sharpening at the rate of 1d. per point. At a hæmatite mine in Cumberland, on the other hand, the miners pay for everything they get, except it be a little waggon grease or a few nails. Again, at a colliery in Lancashire the company does not supply the men with tools, so that they must be bought elsewhere; hence no deductions are necessary under this head; the men also pay their own sharpener, to whom shelter and coal are given by the company. As an intermediate example may be mentioned a hæmatite mine in Furness; here most tools are paid for—spades, hammers, saws, and also dynamite, fuse, and candles—but drill steel is not paid for, neither are picks; and there is no charge for sharpening tools.

At a gold mine on the Rand, all contractors pay for native labour, dynamite, fuse, caps, and candles. Tools are provided free by the company, and sharpening is not charged for.

All the tools and stores delivered to miners are carefully recorded by the storekeeper in a special book, which will be described in Part II. under the head of "Store Books."

A good example of a blacksmith's book is that used at Hodbarrow Mine and is here given:—

No. ....

Date.	Picks.		Hammers.	Guns.*	Scrapers.	Bulls.†	Gads Sharpened.	Tools.	Jumpers Sharpened.			
	Sharpened.	Steeled.								£	s.	d.

The joiner also keeps an account of new handles put into picks and hammers, but a memorandum book suffices for this, or even a board.

The deductions for sharpening and new hilts are sometimes, in Cornwall for instance, brought by the storekeeper into the book in which he records deductions for stores.

It has already been mentioned that in the case of a long bargain, especially

* A simple form of pump used for sucking liquid mud out of holes bored for blasting.
† A pointed bar used for making holes for blasting in stiff clay or similar ground. It is driven in directly with a heavy hammer.

in Cornwall, the amount due to the miner is not carefully ascertained before every pay-day, but a certain sum called "subsist" is paid on account. At the end of the bargain, when the amount is made straight, this subsist comes off as a deduction.

C. **Wages Determined by Value of Mineral Gotten.**—The character of the deductions in this case can be readily seen from the following list of actual deductions made at a Cornish mine:—

Doctor, Club and Barber,*
Materials, Tools, &c.,   } as in Tutwork.
Subsist,
Drawing and Sampling.
Dressing.
Returning charges.

Drawing.—Winding or hoisting the ore in the shaft, charged at 3d. per ton.
Sampling.—Taking a sample and assaying it is charged 1s.
Dressing.—As here used it refers only to a preliminary breaking, charged at from 4d. to 6d. per ton.
Returning charges are the charges for the true dressing operations; they vary from 2s. per ton, in the case of ore which carries 1½ per cent. or less of cassiterite, to 10s. per ton when the ore has 10 per cent. or more of cassiterite.

It will be seen that in addition to the usual deductions which this system has in common with tutwork, the tributer must pay for hoisting and dressing his ore; that is, he pays all charges on it till it is ready for the smelter.

CHAPTER IV.—PAY-SHEETS, DUE-BILLS, AND PAY-TICKETS.

Pay-sheets.—Having considered the various books and forms containing the primary records from which the gross amount of money due to workmen can be calculated, and those in which deductions are recorded, we next pass on to consider the various ways in which these data are set out, so as to ascertain the net amount of money due to the men, preparatory to pay day. Either books or loose sheets may be used; the latter is, perhaps, the more general custom, for books would need to be of such large dimensions as to be very unwieldy.

Classification of the information contained in pay-sheets is of the greatest importance, both for internal comparison and for facilitating the incorporation of the data in the further accounts of a company.

Two forms of sheet are generally used, one for contracts (*bargain-work*), and the other for day-work. The latter generally provides for piece-work also, as men who usually work by the day, not infrequently take a particular job by the piece. On the bargain-work sheets, the miners are classified according to the district they work in; on the other sheets, the first division is into underground and surface workmen; then each of these classes is broken up into groups according to the work the men are engaged in, as explained in speaking of the time-book (see p. 13).

The names of individuals or gangs are written in a vertical column, and there are parallel columns in which are written, opposite each name, the gross amount of money due, the deductions, and the net amount due. The number of columns varies according to the amount of detail desired. Further, the whole, or a part, of a man's wages, from the company's

* At some Cornish mines, in continuance of ancient custom, a barber comes to the mine every Saturday to shave the men; for this he receives 3d. per head per month.

PAY-SHEETS, DUE-BILLS, AND PAY-TICKETS. 27

point of view, may represent money spent in permanent improvements—that is, capital expenditure, which it may be desirable to distinguish from current expenditure connected directly with getting and treating the mineral. This might also be done by the use of vertical columns.

A few examples of forms actually in use may be instructive (see pp. 28, 29). We have, first, examples of the two pay-sheets used at a hæmatite mine in Furness. On the miner's sheet there are columns for the various items for which payment is made, arranged under five heads, and columns for the totals of the items under each head. Next there is a column headed "total earnings," which receives the grand total of the other five totals. Finally, there is provision for deductions, and a column for net amount due. The other sheet needs no comment. Sometimes, as in the next example, there are one or two additional columns at the end, showing average wages earned; but at this particular mine, for convenience of future reference, the average earnings of miners are recorded in a separate book, which is ruled thus :—

AVERAGE WAGES BOOK.

Name of Company.	Name of pit.	No. of men.	Over-time.	Lost time.	Days worked.	Amount earned.	Average per day.
							s. d.

The third example, from Rio Tinto, sufficiently explains itself. The next example is from a colliery in South Wales. The details of money due for dead-work occupy the first set of columns, those for getting coal the next set, then follows a column for the total of these items, and one for the percentage to be taken off or added on; after which are two columns, one for allowances and the other for bonuses, neither of which is subject to the percentage alterations of the other earnings, but is always net cash. Further there is a column for total gross earnings, a set of columns for deductions, and, finally, a column showing the net amount to be paid to the workmen. For convenience in paying, the information contained in the last column is written on a sheet which has consecutive numbers, known as "pay numbers," but which have nothing to do with the numbers by which the miners are known; as each sum is paid, it is ticked off on the sheet; such a sheet is by no means universally used. Special attention should be called to a column headed "total length of heading" in the last pay-sheet. This figure gives the manager a valuable check on yard work, which is often overpaid, for he can scale off these lengths on the plan from time to time.

Where columns are very numerous, as in the last example, reference to the pay-sheets is greatly assisted by a judicious use of coloured inks in printing the forms.

The fifth example is from the Rand. Sometimes the form used for day wages is much simpler than the example (No. 2) given above as, especially in out of the way places, clerk's work is expensive. The following example is from Colorado [*] :—

No.	Name.	Employment.	No. of Days.	Rate.	Amount.	Insurance.	Board.[†]	Net Amount.	Remarks.

[*] I am indebted to both Mr. Bedford M'Neill, A.R.S.M., of London, and Mr. E. Le Neve Foster, of Denver, for forms and information relating to Colorado.
[†] This deduction is paid at once to the boarding-house keeper, and does not go into the accounts of the Company.

EXAMPLES OF

1 MINERS' WAGES, *Fortnight ending May 26, 1894.*

No. of Men.	Names.	Name or No. of pit.	RAISING ORE AND SAND.						BLACK ORE.				MUCK.				Particulars.
			Ore.	Sand.	Rate.		Amount.		No. of Bogies	Rate.	Amount.		No. of Bogies	Rate.	Amount.		
			Tons.	Tons.		£	s.	d.		d.	£	s. d.		d.	£	s. d.	
14	Wm. Jones,	No. 9	223		1/4	14	17	4	107	9	6	5 3	260	7½	8	8 2	Limestone and ore.

2 SURFACE WAGES *for the Fortnight ending*..1S

			DAY WORK.															
No.	Name.	Occupation.	Sunday.	Monday.	Tuesday.	Wednesday.	Thursday.	Friday.	Saturday.	Sunday.	Monday.	Tuesday.	Wednesday.	Thursday.	Friday.	Saturday.	Days.	Rate.	Amount.
																			£ s. d.

3

Contractors.	Place.	Description of work.	Tons.	Measurement.		Trucks.	Price.
				Linear metres.	Cubic metres.		
Joaquin Bañon,	Shaft No. 21,	Driving level,		14·90			Reals. 400
Do.,	,, ,,	,, ,,		13·65			250
José Postigo Jerranimo,	5B to 9B,	Mining and filling ore, Work for mines A/c,	248¾				12

4 LLANBRADACH COLLIERY.

							DEAD WORK.															
Name of district.	Pay number.	Name.	Occupation.	Working number.	Total length of heading.	Headings.		Airways.		Coal carting.		Ripping top.		Cutting bottom.		Props.		Double timber.		Cogs.		Laying partings.
						Yds.	At Amt.	Yds.	At Amt.	Yds.	At Amt.	Yds.	At Amt.	Yds.	At Amt.	No.	At Amt.	No.	At Amt.	No.	At Amt.	No. At Amt.

5 MINE CONTRACTOR'S

Date.	Name.	Working Place.	Latest Measurement.		Paid for		Due.		Price per Foot.		
			Ft.	Ins.	Ft.	Ins.	Ft.	Ins.	£	s.	d.

PAY-SHEETS.

Pay day, June 2, 1894.   *PARK MINES.*

FATHOM WORK.						EXTRA WORK.							Amount.	Total earnings.	DEDUCTIONS.		Total deductions.	Net amount due.
Driving.		Rising.		Reopening.		Amount.	Days.	Rate.	Old wool, 3d.	Saving timber, 6d.	Lining levels, 1s.	Pillars.			Club and Hospital.	Materials.		
Fm.	Ft.	Rate	Fm.	Ft.	Rate	Fm.	Ft.	Rate													
	s.						£	s.	d.					£	s.	d.	£	s.	d.	£	s.	d.	£	s.	d.	£	s.	d.	£	s.	d.
4	0	20					5	18	4		11	14		0	19	6	30	8	7	0	14	0	4	1	0	4	15	0	31	13	7
3	5	10																													

Pay Day...18   *PARK MINES.*

PIECE WORK.				Total Earnings.		DEDUCTIONS.			Amount.		Net amount due.	
Description.	Quantity.	Rate.	Amount.			Rent.	Club and Hospital.	Doctor.				
			£	s.	d.	£	s.	d.			£	s.	d.	£	s.	d.

	Gross amount.		To be deducted.					Pay due.	Shifts worked.		Net wage per man per shift.
Items.	Total	Stores.	Tools repaired and sharpened.	* Work for mines A/c.	Total.			Men.	Boys.	
Reals. 5960 3412 2985 160	Reals. 50	Reals.	Reals.	Reals.	Reals.	Reals.		Reals.		
	9372	50	1693	12	51	70	1744	82	7627	68	366	20	84
	3145		648	50	45	25	144	27	838	2	2306	98	138	16	72

* Paid to another contractor for filling ore.

Pay..................Ending.....................189

COAL.										DEDUCTIONS.					
Turning stalls.	Days.	At	Time. Amt.	Total dead work.	Rate.	Amount.	Total.	Percentage.	On	Off	Allowances.	Bonus.	Gross earnings.	Subs.	Doctor.	Rent.	Coal.	Stores.	Total deductions.	Balance payable.	Pay number.
					Tons.	Cwts.																

PAY BOOK.

Deduct.		At			Amount Deducted.			Gross Amount.			Amount Paid.			Days Worked
No.	Stores.	£	s.	d.	£	s.	d.	£	s.	d.	£	s.	d.	

MINE ACCOUNTS.

The books used in Cornwall connected with the payment of workmen are :—
1. Day-work book.
2. Tutwork ledger.
3. Tribute account book.
4. Cost book.

The first and third are ruled with vertical columns, and need no special description. The tutwork book is kept in the form of a ledger, and will be better understood after Chapter X. has been read. In the example here given it will, however, be readily seen that the gross money due to the miner appears on the right-hand page, and the deduction on the left; and that the "balance" on the left-hand side, necessary to make the sum total of this side equal to that of the right-hand side, is the net amount due to the company of men (*pare*).

TUTWORK LEDGER.

Dr. JOHN JONES. *Cr.*

Date.		£	s.	d.	£	s.	d.	Date.		Tons.	Cwts.	Fms.	Feet.	Ins.	Price.	£	s.	d.
1893.								1893.										
Aug. 19,	To cost,		11	18	2			Sep. 16,	By driving the 420 fms. level east of engine shaft, ,, Sundry repairs to pitwork, two months, .									
Sep. 16,	,,		14	11	0													
						26	9	2										
,, 2,	To subsist, ,, doctor, 29s.; club, 21s. 9d.; barber, 7s. 3d., . Balance, .					75	0	0			7	1	6			£25	181	5	0
																37	2	0
						2	18	0										
						113	19	10										
						218	7	0								218	7	0

When the tutwork "bargain" is per ton of "tinstuff" gotten, the weight of the "stuff" is obtained from the sampling book, for both tutwork and tribute tinstuff are sampled.

The **Cost Book** is the most important book at a Cornish mine. In it the information contained in the above-mentioned three books is brought together. The following is an example :—

Men. Boys. Girls.	Name and Description of work.	Tons.	Cwts.	Fathoms.	Feet.	Inches.	Price.	Amount.			Total Amount.			Subsist.			Materials.			Doctor.	Club.	Barber.	Balance.	To whom paid.
								£	s.	d.	£	s.	d.	£	s.	d.	£	s.	d.				£	s.	d.
15	John Jones and prs. driving 420 fms. level east from shaft, . . Sundry repairs to pitwork, ...	7	1	6			25	181	5	0															
								37	2	0	218	7	0	75	0	0	20	0	2	29/	21/9	7/3	113	19	10

In addition to wages, the cost book contains other matters (see p. 114).

Due-Bills and Pay-Tickets.—It is usual to give full details to the men working on contract, so that they can see exactly how the net amount due to them has been arrived at. This information is sometimes given on pay-day, but it is often supplied a day or two previously, in order to enable partners to make beforehand the necessary calculations for the division of their money.

PAY-SHEETS, DUE-BILLS, AND PAY-TICKETS. 31

The tickets used in the latter case are known as **due-bills**. The following is an example of the form given by a colliery to the miners :—

..................................COLLIERIES CO., LD.,*
........................COLLIERY.

No. 801.   Name, Wm. Rees.   Working No. 64.
Occupation, Collier.   Pay, ending....................189

	Trams.	T.	C.	Rate.	£	s.	d.	£	s.	d.
Large Coal, . .	20	11		1/6	1	10	9			
1. Headings, 3 Shifts,			3	3/-		9				
2. Airways, 2 ,,				2/3						
3. Stalls, 2 ,,				/9						
4. Coal Carting, .				/8						
5. Ripping Top, .			3	/2			6			
6. Cutting Bottom,			3	3/-		9				
7. Props, .				/5						
8. Double Timber,				1/-						
9. Cogs, .				1/-						
10. Laying Partings,				2/-						
11. Turning Stalls,				5/-						
12. Days, .										
TOTAL,					2	9	3			
Add 18¾ per cent., .						9	2			
Allowance or Bonus,						10				
GROSS EARNINGS,								3	8	5
DEDUCTIONS:—										
Cash Advanced,										
Sick Fund, .						1				
Rent, .										
Coal, .										
Stores, .						7				
Check Weigher,								1	7	
This Ticket must be presented for payment before 2.30 p.m. on Pay Day.					PAY	3	6	10			

No. 801.   Cash at Pay   3   6   10
                                        Deductions   1   7

Date............   Pay £   3   8   5

* The following explanation of terms used in the account has been kindly furnished by Prof. Galloway :—

The cutting price of 1s. 6d. per ton is payable without addition when men are working one shift of 8 or 10 hours' duration in places 8 yards or more in width. When two shifts or three shifts are worked in 24 hours, some of the men have to work by night, and, occasionally, also the men who constitute one shift have to leave before they have completed all the work they wish to do, so as to make room for the next shift. Both of these contingencies are considered unfavourable to the workmen, and hence a certain allowance per yard driven is made to compensate for the real or supposed disadvantage.

1. *Headings* are main roadways driven for haulage purposes, in which part of the roof (*top*) is taken down, or part of the floor (*bottom*) is "raised" to give the necessary height. They are not so wide as stalls—and an allowance of 3s. per yard is made when three shifts are worked.

2. *Airways* are still narrower than headings, as a rule; but they do not require the roof or floor to be cut.

MINE ACCOUNTS.

On pay-day the collier tears off the slip at the bottom, and handing it to the pay-clerk, receives the cash due to him; thus the slips enable the pay to go on smoothly and quickly, and at the same time serve as acknowledgments from the men that they have received the money owing to them.

At the same colliery the following is the form of due-bill given to labourers (*day men*):—

.... COLLIERIES CO., LTD.

.... COLLIERY.

No................ Name,..

Occupation,..Pay, ending....................189

			£	s.	d.	£	s.	d.
Days . .	@ . .							
Add . .	. per cent.							
Days . .	@ . .							
Add . .	. per cent.							
Bonus,	. .							
Gross Earnings, .								
DEDUCTIONS:—								
Cash Advanced (Sub),	.							
Sick Fund, . . .	.							
Rent, ...	.							
Coal, ...	.							
Stores, . . .	.							
			PAY					

No...............   Cash at Pay
                                     Deductions
Date,......................   **Pay £**

3. *Stalls* are the ordinary wide working-places in which the bulk of the coal is worked.
4. *Coal Carting.*—In the airways and in some of the stalls in which the roof and floor are left intact, the height is insufficient to admit of the ordinary mine waggons being taken to the face. The coal is then filled into a small waggon carrying 5 or 6 cwts., and conveyed from the face to the point at which the larger mine waggon is standing, and is there transferred to the larger waggon. This involves a certain amount of extra work to the collier, and is paid for at the rate of 8d. per yard driven forward in a stall producing, say, 25 tons of coal per yard forward.
5. *Ripping Top* (taking down roof).—2d. per inch per yard forward for a width of 6 feet in rock—that is to say, 2 square yards 1 inch thick, 2d. Suppose the thickness to be 3 feet of hard rock, then the cost would be 6s. for 2 cubic yards, or 3s. per cubic yard.
6. *Cutting Bottom* ("raising floor").—Where the floor is softer than the roof, additional height is generally obtained by cutting away the former. 3s. per yard forward and 6 feet wide is then paid—that is to say, 1d. for 2 square yards 1 inch thick.
7. *Props.*—Single uprights for supporting the roof at the side of the roadway.
8. *Double Timber.*—Two uprights and one cross timber resting upon the uprights.
9. *Cogs.*—Timbers laid crossways two and two, so as to form a small pillar 3 feet or 4 feet square.
10. *Laying Partings.*—Putting in a set of points and crossings.
11. *Turning Stalls.*—A stall is worked at right angles to a heading. When the stall is commenced, the men are liable to be inconvenienced and delayed by the passing traffic. After the coal has been removed to a distance of 8 or 10 feet from the heading, and the roof

It is not usual to give due-bills to men paid by the day.
The next example shows a **due-bill** in the form of an account; it will be further noticed that this example shows every detail of gross money due, and all stores charged against the men. Originally a simpler form was employed at this mine; but, at the request of the men for fuller details, the form below was designed, and it has given general satisfaction. The right-hand side is filled up by the storekeeper; the left-hand side is copied from the pay-sheet:—

........................CO., LTD.

Dr. ....MINES PAY.   *Fortnight ending* 26*th May*, 1894.   Cr.

WILLIAM JONES & CO., 14 MEN.	Rate.	£ s. d.		Rate.	£ s. d.	£ s. d.
No. 9 Pit.						
Raising 223 tons Ore,	1/4	14 17 4	Candles,.........56 lbs.,	/6	1 8 0	
Do. 269 Bogies Muck,......	/7½	8 8 2	Dynamite,.........4 lbs.,	7/6	1 10 0	
Do. 167 Bogies Black Ore,	/9	6 5 3	Gelatine,...........1 lb.	8/	0 8 0	
....			Fuse,............6 coils,	1/	0 6 0	
Fathoms. Ft. Ins.			Detonators,........1 box,	4/	0 4 0	
Driving, 4	20/	4 0 0	Spades,...............		0 2 6	
Do., 3 5	10/	1 18 4	Pick Shafts,........5 @	/6	0 2 6	
Rising,						
Do., ...						4 1 0
Re-opening,......						
Do., ...			Club and Hospital, ...			0 14 0
......Days.			Rent, ...			
Old Wood,...............Bogies,						
Timber,..................11 Pieces,	/6	0 5 6				
Lining Levels,........14 Courses,	1/	0 14 0				4 15 0
Pillars,...................................						
....			Cash due,...............			31 13 7
		36 8 7				36 8 7

To facilitate the operation of paying the men, on the morning of the pay-day, the monies due are counted out and placed upon tickets, on which have been previously written the names of the gangs and the net amounts respectively due to them, as in the example below.

........................MINES.

No. 9 *Pit.*   2*nd June*, 1894.

WILLIAM JONES & CO., 14 MEN.

£31 : 13 : 7

When all the money is ready, the names of the men are called out one after the other, and the money handed over to them. A slightly different ticket is used for men paid by the day; it shows deductions, as they receive no due-bill. It is as follows :—

---

has been taken down or the floor cut away to give the necessary height, the "parting" (consisting of two points and a crossing) is laid in the railway in the headway, and a waggon can then be brought into the stall. Before this is done, the waggon into which the coal is filled must stand on the railway in the heading. Sometimes also the stall is commenced with a width of only 6 or 7 feet, and carried for some distance away from the heading at that width, and afterwards widened out in the coal. For these disadvantages a sum of 5s. is allowed.

12. *Days.*—The men are occasionally employed at so much per day in doing work, such as cutting small faults, removing falls of roof, &c., which are not embraced in any of the categories given above.

..........................MINES.

June 2, 1894.

John Pyne,	. . .	£2 15 11
Club and Hospital, .	.	0 1 0
		£2 14 11

The useful practice is followed at the Foxdale Mine, Isle of Man, of having the men's accounts written pay by pay into small books ruled for the purpose, so that, by looking in the earlier pages of their books, the men can see what they have been earning in the previous months. Of course men can keep their due-bills or pay-tickets, but this plan is not so convenient as having them bound together in a book. When due-bills are not given to workmen, their pay-tickets should contain full details showing how the amount of money due has been calculated. It may be mentioned that bags, envelopes, and small tin boxes are frequently used instead of tickets in paying. A form like one or other of those given above may be printed on the backs of the envelopes; the tin boxes are usually numbered.

PART II.

PURCHASES AND SALES.

CHAPTER V.—PURCHASE AND DISTRIBUTION OF STORES.

Stores.—Under the head of "stores" are included the numerous and very various articles and goods which it is necessary for a mining company to buy in order to carry on operations. They are sold according to different units. Thus iron and steel are sold by the ton; spikes, nails and screws by the cwt.; spades, saws, axes and hammers by the dozen; oils by the gallon; greases and tallow by the cwt.; cotton waste by the cwt.; candles by the dozen lbs.; gunpowder by the 100 lbs. and the cwt.; dynamite by the ton of 2,000 lbs.; fuse by the coil of 24 feet; caps by the 1,000; and ropes, whether made of iron or steel wire, or hemp, by the cwt. Coal was, until recently, sold by the ton of 21 cwts.; but now, because of altered railway rates, it is generally sold in Britain by the statute ton of 20 cwts.

Different classes of timber are sold according to different units. Round timber is most frequently sold by the cubic foot, as estimated from **string measure**—that is to say, the length of the piece is multiplied by a fourth of the girth squared to obtain the cubic contents. Square timber, on the other hand, is sold by the cubic foot, **caliper measure**—that is to say, the length of the piece is multiplied by the square of the side to obtain the cubic contents —or if, as is usually the case, two adjacent sides are not quite equal in length, they are both measured.

Round timber slightly squared may be sold either by **string** or by **caliper** measure; the latter method is more frequent, but in this case the buyer must not forget that he is nominally paying for more timber than he gets. On the other hand, the volume as estimated by string measure is less than the actual content. A "load" of timber is 50 cubic feet, and a "standard" of round timber is sometimes given as 100 cubic feet, while a "standard" of partly round timber is 150 cubic feet.* These standards are comparatively little used. Props are sometimes sold by length, the diameter being specified within certain limits, and sometimes by the ton; Irish larch, for instance, is generally sold by the ton in the north of England.

Occasionally mining companies buy a wood or forest of standing timber.

Planks are sold wholesale by the "standard"; the St. Petersburg standard (165 cubic feet) being the one most generally used. The number of superficial feet in a standard is found by multiplying 165 by the ratio of 12 inches to

* Merivale, *Notes and Formulæ for Mining Students*. 3rd ed. London, 1890, p. 26.
See also Haworth's *Practical Timber Measurer*. 3rd ed. Liverpool, 1895.

the thickness of the planks. Thus, in the case of 3-inch planks the number of superficial feet in a standard is $165 \times \frac{12}{3} = 660$. So that in measuring a waggon-load of 3-inch "deals" the length and breadth of each plank would be taken and multiplied together; and the sum of these products divided by 660 would give the number of standards.

Smaller quantities of planks, especially small planks or boards, are sold per 100 **superficial** feet.

In America, timber used for firing is cut into 4 feet lengths and sold by the "cord," which is a pile of timber 4 feet × 4 feet × 8 feet. In selling other timber, the unit employed is 1,000 feet "board" measure; *i.e.*, 1,000 superficial feet 1 inch thick. Thus, 500 cubic feet of timber is 6,000 feet board measure.

Stores are ordered and paid for from the office of a Mining Company; hence the books connected with these transactions are kept there, as also are the summaries and analyses of stores received and of stores used. The books connected with the details of receipt and distribution of goods are of course kept at the store on the mine. The storekeeper is chiefly concerned with **quantities**; it is his business to see that the stock on hand equals the goods received, less the goods distributed; while the monetary matters connected with the stores are managed in the office.

The books and forms connected with stores can be conveniently considered under three heads:—(A) Those relating to the purchase of stores; (B) those relating to the receipt and distribution of stores; (C) those connected with balancing stores received and used and stock.

A. **Books and Forms Relating to the Purchase of Stores.—Requisitions.**—Requisitions for stores required are sent from the store, either as the goods are wanted, or, more generally, at regular intervals, such as a month. They are, as a rule, written on a sheet of foolscap; but special forms are also used. The following is an example:—*

..................................MINE, ...*189*

A supply of the undermentioned articles is required.

Article.	Purpose.	Date of Last Supply.	Quantity of Last Supply.	By whom Supplied.	Rate of Last Supply.	Present Stock.	Remarks.

Quotations and Contracts.—Generally quotations are requested, at intervals, for such goods as are regularly used at mines; and, to secure uniformity, printed forms may very conveniently be sent to merchants. The following is an example of such a form as would be sent to an oil merchant:—

* Adapted from Garcke & Fells' *Factory Accounts.* 4th ed. London, 1893, p. 45.

PURCHASE AND DISTRIBUTION OF STORES.

From
.............MINING CO., LD.
............189

To.......................................

Please quote your price for the undernoted goods, delivered at ....Station, ...Railway, less 2½ per cent., cash one month.

Description	Price	
	s.	d.
Best Engine Oil,			Per gall.
Common Engine Oil,			,,
Lubricine (Cylinder Oil),			,,
Bogie Oil,			,,
Lucigen Oil,			,,
Paraffin ,,			,,
Colza ,,			,,
Castor ,,			,,
Wire Rope Oil,			,,
Bogie Grease,			Per cwt.
Tallow,			,,
Soft Soap,			,,
White Lead,			,,
Red ,,			,,
Cotton Waste,			,,

At the particular mine where this form is used, a second printed form is kept for quotations from hardware merchants, and a blank form for miscellaneous requirements.

Another method is to send out schedules of requirements and to request tenders. There are two cases :—(i.) Where a tender is requested for a particular article or lot of goods; and (ii.) where a tender is requested for the regular supply of certain goods for a period of six or twelve months.

Tenders differ from quotations only in being more formal. When a request is made for a tender, various instructions and conditions are given and a form of tender is appended.

Contracts are almost invariably made for the supply of the principal regular requirements of a mine for 6 or 12 months; *e.g.*, timber, dynamite, perhaps candles, and certainly coal in the case of a metalliferous mine. Even for the supply of such things as oils and cotton waste, it is a good thing to contract, or accept a tender for a period, as generally a little is saved thereby; while the manager is relieved from the trouble of constant buying, and is more at liberty to devote his time to his other duties.

Contract notes consist of two parts, one retained by the buyer, the other by the seller, the part held by the buyer being signed by the seller and *vice versâ*. The following is a typical example :—

..................................18......

RECORD OF CONTRACT MADE.

Bought of M..

....

Price..

....

Delivery...

....

Payment ....

STRIKES, &c.—In case of strikes, accidents, difficulties with workmen, short supply of waggons, or other unavoidable circumstances causing the stoppage or partial stoppage of Works, or otherwise interfering with the manufacture or delivery of the material now contracted for, deliveries may be suspended or partially suspended during such interruptions, and the period of the contract extended accordingly. This clause applies equally to buyers and sellers.

..................................(Address).

..................................18......

RECORD OF CONTRACT MADE.

Sold to M..

....

Price..

....

Delivery...

....

Payment ....

STRIKES, &c.—In case of strikes, accidents, difficulties with workmen, short supply of waggons, or other unavoidable circumstances causing the stoppage or partial stoppage of Works, or otherwise interfering with the manufacture or delivery of the material now contracted for, deliveries may be suspended or partially suspended during such interruptions, and the period of the contract extended accordingly. This clause applies equally to buyers and sellers.

When any plant is bought, such as a steam engine, it is usually contracted for according to drawings and specifications supplied by the engineer of the mine.

In purchasing ordinary stores, quotations or tenders generally specify $2\frac{1}{2}$ per cent. discount for payment within a month. In Cornwall 5 per cent. is allowed for payment within a month, and $2\frac{1}{2}$ per cent. for payment within three or four months. If payment is not made within these periods, all discount is lost.

Orders.—The requisition having been received from the mine, and the quotations, or accepted tenders, of the merchants being to hand, an order is made out for the goods required. Orders ought always to be made out on a special form and signed by the manager or secretary of a company. These forms are generally numbered and bound in a book with counterfoils.

Invoices and Payment of Accounts.—The goods having been dispatched, an invoice is sent by the merchant to the mining company. This may simply contain details of the goods which have been sent, in which case

PURCHASE AND DISTRIBUTION OF STORES.

it is often called an "advice note"; but such is only used where quantities of the same class of goods are being sent at frequent intervals, as in the case of timber. An invoice generally contains, in addition to details of the goods which have been forwarded, an account of the money owing for them.

In some cases the invoice is sent from the mining company's office to the mine store to be checked. This, however, is not a good practice. It is much better to have an account of all goods received sent to the office, and to have the invoice checked there.

Goods are usually paid for at regular intervals, generally once a month. In the case where advice notes* have been sent with goods, monthly accounts showing the money due for goods delivered, are sent out by merchants. These are checked by means of the advice notes, which have already been corrected; then the percentage allowed is deducted, and the net amount due to each merchant is ascertained.

Where invoices are sent, of course, no monthly accounts are necessary.

In the case of a company, the various accounts owing may be set out in a tabular form to receive the sanction of the directors for their payment. The following is an example of such a form :—

.... MINING COMPANY, LIMITED.

ACCOUNTS FOR PAYMENT, MONTH OF ...., 189...

The following Accounts have been certified as correct and passed for payment :—

Dept.	To whom Payable.	Gross Amount of Account.	Discount.	Contra Accounts and other Deductions.	Net Amount.	Total net Amount for which cheque is to be drawn.	Amount for which Bill is to be drawn.	Secretary's Initials.	Directors' Initials.	Remarks.

After this cheques are written out, signed by one or two directors and the secretary, or by some authorised person, and forwarded. It is not nowadays usual to send with the money the actual accounts or invoices to be receipted. Generally a note of explanation on a printed form, together with, perhaps, a form of receipt, is enclosed with the cheque.

The invoices should always be kept. They may be pasted in a guard book for preservation. In this book they are folded so as to occupy less space, and in such a way that they can be easily referred to. The names of the merchants and amounts of the account are written on the fold exposed to view, or they are numbered consecutively with the page of the "journal" (see p. 87) on which they are recorded when they enter the general accounts of the company, as thus :—

No.	Folio of Journal
175.	27.

A rubber stamp may be conveniently used for impressing this form upon

* The deduction for percentage allowed or discount is usually deducted at head office.

the back of the invoice. Another method is to have a guard-book with pages wider than the invoices, and two columns on the right-hand side—one for the name of the merchant, and the other for the amount of the invoice. An index to the names of merchants is generally prepared. Some persons object altogether to a guard-book on account of its clumsiness, and simply file the invoices. The receipts are likewise numbered consecutively and filed, or pasted in a guard book and indexed.

Information relative to requisitions, orders, and invoices may be tabulated for convenience of future reference. One example is as follows [*]:—

Date of Requisition.	Goods Required.	Wanted by	Purpose.	To be Ordered from	Order.		Invoice.		Remarks.
					No.	Rate.	Amount Due.		

Another example in use is the following:—

ORDER BOOK.

Date Ordered.	Order No.	By whom Ordered.	Particulars of Goods Ordered.	Price.	Date Received.	For which Mine.[†]	Conditions of Purchase.	Remarks.

Sometimes a copy of all the invoices is made in a book ruled with columns, especially in cases where the chief office of a company is at some distance from the mine; the invoices are kept at the chief office and the copy at the office on the mine.

B. **Books and Forms relating to the Receipt and Distribution of Stores.**—Receipt of Stores.—Sometimes the receipt of stores is notified daily to the office. This may be done on forms bound together in a book with counterfoils, but a better method is to obtain a duplicate by using carbon paper. The following example shows such a form:—

PARK MINES,
Goods received this.......day of............189...

Waggon No.	Whom or Where from.	No. of Articles.	Description.	Weight.			Remarks.
				Tons.	cwts.	qrs. lbs.	

.... *Storekeeper.*

Another method is to enter all stores received into a book, which is sent to the office at intervals so that invoices can be checked and more permanent records made. The ruling might be similar to that of the above example.

---

[*] Garcke and Fells, *Op. cit.*, p. 46.
[†] The company using this form works three mines.

PURCHASE AND DISTRIBUTION OF STORES.

The more permanent record of stores received generally includes their cost and sometimes an analysis. The following example is from Llanbradach Colliery :—

Left-hand page.

Date.	From Whom.	Number.	Article.	Weight.				Rate.	Amount of items.		
				Tons.	Cwt.	Qrs.	Lbs.		£	s.	d.

Right-hand page.

Total Amount.	Ledger Folio.	Pit-wood.	Sleepers and Rails.	Iron, Steel, and Castings.	General Stores.	Oils.	Lime, Bricks, Timber.	Electric Goods.	Duplicate Machinery.

The total cost of stores at the mine, which is the important figure for a mining company to know, is not always, as in England, what is paid to the merchant. Freight, duty, &c., may have to be added. The following is an example from Kimberley of a "stores-received" book, with provision for setting forth each item of cost :—

Order No.	Date of Invoice.	Date Received.	Nos. of Packages.	Ledger Folios.	Particulars.	First Cost.	Freight, &c.	Duty, &c.	Carriage.	Total Cost at Works.

Distribution of Stores.—Workmen are frequently allowed to obtain goods from the store merely on asking for what they want. This is a bad system, for besides the lack of any check, and the possibility of fraud, it is notorious that workmen, though used to making a little go a long way at home, are often grossly extravagant when dealing with what they do not have to pay for. Therefore it is best to arrange that stores shall only be given out on the production of an order to the storekeeper signed by an authorised person; even in the case of contract men, who pay for the stores they get, it is best to insist on this, for it must be remembered that the miners' average wages are calculated from the *net* amount, not the *gross* amount of money paid to them, and that deducting the value of stores is only a device for making men more careful; their cost really falls upon the mining company. The order tickets are usually numbered and duplicated; sometimes a form with counterfoil is used, or, better, a copy is made by using carbon paper. The following is an example :—

MINE ACCOUNTS.

NOTE FOR MATERIALS.   No. ....

.... COLLIERY COMPANY, LIMITED.

.... COLLIERIES.

To the Storekeeper. 189

Please supply Bearer with the following :—

No.	Description.	Where to be Used.
		Revenue or Capital A/c.

Signed....................

As a rule, orders are not given for timber, which is taken as required, and sometimes this is also the case with iron and steel. At the De Beers Mines, however, special red tickets are given by authorised persons for timber and green tickets for firewood, the tickets for other stores being white. At a colliery in South Wales the banksman keeps an account, by weight, of all the timber that goes down the pit, and also of everything else, in the way of stores and materials, which passes through his hands. Thus, although order-tickets are not used for timber, a check on consumption and stocks is obtained.

Stores are generally given out at specified hours each day. After each delivery, detailed records should be made, in a book or books, of every item delivered, the order tickets serving as a guide. At some mines no record is kept of those stores delivered which are charged against the mine, but only of those which are paid for by men working on contract. This is not a good practice, though it is useful to keep a separate book for goods delivered which are paid for by the miners.

The following is an example of a Cornish "stores-delivery" book, for items with which the men are charged ; it also contains columns for blacksmith's cost and for the deduction for sampling and drawing :—

....................MINE, Men's Cost for

Takers' Names.	Candles.	Fuse.	Powder.	Gelatine.*	Dynamite.	Caps.	Small Hilts.	Large Hilts.	Cans and Locks.	Shovels and Axes.	Small Kegs.
	4d.	6d.	6d.	1s.	9d.	3s.	4d.	8d.	1s.	2s. 6d.	2s. 6d.
John Smith,	30	5		80				1			
	30	15		20		100	1				1/6
	30	6		20						1	
	30	6		20		100					1/6
	120	32		140		200	1	1		1	
	40/-	16/-		140/-		6/-	4d.	8d.		2/6	3/

* Blasting-gelatine.

PURCHASE AND DISTRIBUTION OF STORES. 43

Continuation :—

4 Weeks ending *August 19, 1893.*

Large Kegs.	Slings.	Clay.	Smith's Cost.	Total Cost of Materials.			Drawing and Samples.			Total Month's Cost.			Ledger Folio.
7s. 6d.	6d.	3d.											
		16 4/-	1	5	8	11	18	2		11	18	2	14

At a hæmatite mine in Furness two books are kept, one for stores-delivered charged against the men, and the other for those charged against the Company. They are respectively ruled thus :—

JOHN JONES & CO. 482

Date.	Quantity.		Description of Material.	Folio of Store Book.	Rate.		Candles.		Dynamite, &c.		Tools.		Total.			Date.	Quantity.	
1893. July 12	No.	lbs. 40	Candles,	20	/6	*s.* 20	*d.*	*s.*	*d.*	*s.*	*d.*	*s.* 1	*d.* 0	*s.* 0	*d.* 0		No.	lbs.
		4	Dynamite,	28	1/9			7	0			0	7	0				
	1		Fuse,		1/-			1	0			0	1	0				
	½		Caps,		3/6			0	10½			0	0	10½				
		4	4-inch steel nails,															
		2	Plate nails,															
		8	Td. rope,															
	1		Dyn. can,		2/-			2	0	0	0	2	0					
	1		Axe,		3/-			3	0	0	3	0						
	2		Pick shafts,		/6			1	0	0	1	0						
						20		8	10½	0		1	14	10½				

It will be observed that there is a column in which each item is recorded, then three columns in which the items are analysed. The money columns are for the amounts which are charged against the men.

No. 9 WINDING ENGINE. 179.

Date.	Quantity.		Description of Material.	Folio of Stores Book.	Date.	Quantity.		Description of Material.	Folio of Stores Book.
1893. July	12	No. 2⅓ 2 1 2	Lbs. gals.	Lubricene. Waste. Oil kettle. Soft soap.	782		No.	Lbs.	

In this form there are columns for quantities, but none for money. Both books are written up by the storekeeper from the order tickets.

The book used for recording stores-delivered which are charged against the mine may be ruled in such a way as to present an analysis of consumption, which is useful in making analyses of costs. The following example from Llanbradach Colliery will illustrate this method :—

Where Used.	Pitwood.			Electric Goods.			Oils.		
	Timber.	Norway Props.	Sleepers.	Iron.	Steel.	Lamps. Holders.	Valvoline Cylinder.	Olive.	&c., &c.
	C. Qr.			Lbs.	Lbs.		Gals. Qts. Pts.	Gals. Qts. Pts.	
No. 1 Winding Engine, No. 2 ,, Air Compressor, Boilers, . &c., &c.									

This book is made up each day, and a weekly analysis is also made (see p. 71).

C. **Books connected with Balancing Stores used and Stock.**—The difference between the amount received and amount delivered of each article gives the stock which ought to be in the mine store. It is important to ascertain this figure accurately in order that the estimated stock may be compared with the actual stock and a check be thus established; besides it is useful for indicating when a new supply of any particular article should be ordered. For ascertaining and recording the balance of goods in store, a stores book, often called a **stores ledger**, is kept, in which a certain portion is allotted to each article, the name of the article being written at the top of the page, and underneath the amount received balanced against the amount delivered. The following is an example :—

Dr.   Candles.   *Cr.*

Date.		Sender.	Weight Received.	Date.			Daily Consumption.	Monthly Consumption.
			lbs.					
1893 July	11	To stock brought forward,	} 200	1893 July	12	{ F 482, 40 lbs.; { F 483, 24 do.;		
,,	12	To J. Hodgson, .	816					

The quantities received are always entered on the left-hand side of the page and the deliveries on the right.

This book is written up by the store's auditor, storekeeper, or other person instructed so to do, who first checks the stores-delivered books (see p. 43) from the duplicates in the order-book kept in the office. F482, 40 lbs. means that on p. 482 of the stores-delivery book, a delivery of 40 lbs. of candles is recorded as having taken place on July 12th. On referring to the stores-delivery books, it will be seen that a column is provided for the folio of the ledger on which the delivery of each article is recorded, so that there is no difficulty in tracing an entry from one book to the other.

The stores ledger is balanced as often as stock is taken. It is almost impossible to avoid small differences occurring in some articles, but every means of tracing the error should be at once adopted.

At Llanbradach, instead of a single book, two books are kept, one for receipts,

PURCHASE AND DISTRIBUTION OF STORES. 45

the other for deliveries. A monthly summary is made in a smaller book, the character of which is shown by the following example :—

PITWOOD.

Date.			Tons.	Cwt.	Stock. Tons.	Cwt.	
Jan.	1	Stock, ...	71	—	71	—	—
		Received during month,	263	—			
		Total, . .	334	—			—
		Consumption, .	240	—			—
Feb.	1	Stock, ...	94	—	94	—	—

Sometimes separate store-books are kept for coal and timber, and occasionally for iron and steel, as these cannot very conveniently be passed through the store-books in the ordinary way. The following is a good example of a "coal" book from Cornwall :—

Left-hand Page.

COALS CONSUMED.

Date.	Engine.	Stamps.	Whim.	Man-Engine, and Compressor.	Calciner.	Smiths.	Sundries.	Total.	Remarks.
	Tons cwt.	Tons cwt.	Tons cwt.	Tons cwt.	Tons cwt.	Tons cwt.	Tons cwt.	Tons cwt.	

Right-hand Page.

COALS RECEIVED.

Merchant.	Quantity.	
	Tons.	Cwt.

[*Lower down page.*]

Quantity received from Merchants this month,
Stock in Coal Yard on First of month, . .

Total, ...
Less consumed, as shown on other side,

Stock in Coal Yard on Last of month,

The coal consumed is entered daily; and weekly totals are made, a page being large enough to record the consumption for a month.

Stock-Taking.—Stock-taking is sometimes done every month; six months is a more frequent interval; and still more commonly stock is only taken once a year. A rough memorandum book is used in the actual operation, and afterwards a classified list is written up in a "stock" book.

CHAPTER VI.—SALE OF PRODUCT.

IN the preceding chapter the Mining Company was the buyer; in this one it is the seller; hence many of the operations described there need only be reversed to apply here.

Minerals go into the market in very different stages of elaboration; thus hæmatite and other iron ores are generally sold to the smelter just as they come from the mine; coal may be sold as it comes from the pit, or it may be screened and picked, or washed, or coked, or made into briquettes; tin ores go through a costly process of dressing, so that the percentage of metal is raised from some $1\frac{1}{2}$ or 2 per cent. to 70 per cent. On the other hand, copper ores often undergo very little preparation for the market, and as sold may contain only 5 or 6 per cent. of copper. Gold is generally sold in ingots, which always contain a little silver and traces of other metals.

Frequently a Mining Company smelts its own ores, and so has only a finished product to put on the market. In this case, however, it is very important that the ore passed to the smelting works should always be credited to the mine at a fair price; otherwise it would not be possible to localise profit or loss, and efficiently superintend the works.

Methods of Sale.—Contract.—Minerals are not infrequently sold by contract; for instance, coal, iron, and manganese ores, and occasionally lead and other ores are so sold. A form of contract-note has already been given (p. 38). It is sometimes agreed that coal shall not have more than a certain percentage of ash, or less than a certain calorific power; but frequently it is simply specified by name. In the case of iron ores, the percentage of iron may be stated in the contract-note, especially in buying foreign ores; but in buying from a local mine, the quality being fairly uniform, the ore is often bought at a price determined by the buyer's previous experience, no percentage composition being guaranteed.

Tender.—Tenders for the sale or the purchase of minerals, are frequently made. There are two cases:—in the first the Mining Company offers to supply a certain quantity of mineral to purchasers, under specified conditions; this is frequently done in the sale of coal, and sometimes in the sale of iron ores; in the other case, which is peculiar to certain ores, the smelters tender for the ore to the mining company; this is the case with lead, silver, tin and copper ores, and gold ores when they are sold as such.

At the Foxdale Mine in the Isle of Man a parcel of ore having been made ready for sale, a sample is sent to the various smelters known to the Company with the following form :—

SALE OF PRODUCT.

ISLE OF MAN MINING COMPANY, LIMITED.

FOXDALE MINES, ISLE OF MAN.

Sampling of .... Tons of Silver-Lead Ore Lying in Ramsey.

TENDERS to be sent in to.. Chester, before Four o'clock p.m., on...when the purchasers will at once be declared; and it is requested that they be marked "*Tender for Ore,*" on the outside.

CONDITIONS OF SALE.

The Highest Tender to be accepted; and should two be alike, and neither withdrawn, the Lot to be divided. *The Purchaser to employ an Agent to check the weighing of the Ore, and to see it shipped into a vessel in Ramsey Harbour;* and the Ore to be at the risk of the Purchasers from the time of such shipment. The Purchasers to clear out the whole Lot at the same time, and within ten days of the date of Sale.

Weight: 20 Cwt. (of 112 lbs. each) to the Ton. Dry Weight.

Payment due on day of Sale, and payable one-half by Cash, and the remainder by an approved Acceptance in London at two months' date; or by Cash at purchaser's option, being allowed interest at the rate of Five per cent. per annum.

(Signed) ....

The value of the ore is ascertained by assaying it, and finding out the amount of lead and silver in it, for silver is always present in lead ores, and is paid for when it exceeds 4 ozs. per ton; deductions are then made for loss in smelting, for cost of smelting, and for carriage. The amount of moisture is ascertained by drying a sample, and the calculated dry weight is the basis of payment.

In buying non-argentiferous lead ores in Missouri,[*] the smelter simply inspects the parcel, and, estimating its value by the eye, makes a bid based on previous experience; but in Colorado, where the ores are frequently rich in silver, and often carry gold, the bids are in the form of an elaborate tariff, setting forth the scale of payment for the various contents of the several classes of ore, based upon New York quotations for the metals contained in them. For example, the general price-list for lead carbonate ores during 1885 was [†]:—

Silver: New York quotation, less 5 per cent.
Gold: $19 per ounce if over 0·1 ounce per ton.
Lead: 45 cents per unit[‡] when the New York quotation of lead is 4·25 cents per lb.; 40 cents per unit when the New York quotation of lead is under 4·25 cents.
The working charges per ton of 2,000 lbs., dry weight, ranged from $3 to $8, according as the percentage of lead varied from 30 to under 10 per cent. There were six other classes of ore for which the scales varied.

In the case of tin and copper ores in Cornwall, the sales are at regular intervals, and are known as "ticketings." Although the glory of the copper ticketings is already "a tale that is told," the tin ticketings are still held every fortnight at Redruth. Previous to these meetings, samples of the lots of ore to

[*] *Engineering and Mining Journal of New York,* July 4th, 1885, p. 4.
[†] *Mineral Resources of the United States,* 1885, p. 251; see also Hofman, *Metallurgy of Lead,* New York, 1892, p. 73; *Engineering and Mining Journal of New York,* vol. li., 1891, p. 85; and Furman, "Purchasing Silver, Gold, and Lead Ores," *School of Mines Quarterly,* vol. xv., 1893-94, p. 1.
[‡] 1 per cent., or 20 lbs. lead to the ton of 2,000 lbs. avoirdupois.

be offered have been sent to the smelters, and they or their representatives come prepared to make bids. A chairman is appointed from among the sellers, and they all sit round a table ; as each lot of ore is called, offers are written on slips of paper (**tickets**, hence the name), and passed up to the chairman, who reads them out, the highest bidder getting the parcel.

The value of the tin ore is ascertained by a dry assay ; the proportion of metal is not stated as a percentage, but as so many cwt. to the ton; thus, 65 per cent. ore would be said to have a "produce" of 13. $1\frac{1}{4}$ is always deducted from the produce for cost of smelting and loss (*returning charges*). Thus, suppose a smelter takes £70 per ton of metallic tin as the basis of his offer, the value of 13 produce ore would be £70 × $(13 - 1\frac{1}{4})$. In weighing the ore on delivery, 3 lbs. per cwt. is allowed off the net weight. The amount taken by the smelter as the basis of calculation is known as the "standard."

Copper ores are sold per ton of 21 cwts. in a similar way to tin ores, but the returning charges are taken at so much per ton of ore instead of reducing the produce by a definite amount.*

Zinc ores are also sold by tender. The methods used in arriving at their value are often complicated. The rule used at Swansea is as follows :†—From 100 deduct the calcination loss, and divide the zinc-content (by assay), less unity and multiplied by 100, by the result. From $\frac{1}{5}$ths of the answer deduct 1. Multiply this remainder by the London quotation price for spelter per ton, less £1, and divide by 100. Deduct returning charges for smelting, £2, 10s.; also deduct calcination-percentage or loss-value, and also 5s. per ton cost of calcination. Suppose a calamine ore assaying 40 per cent. zinc, with a calcination loss of 30 per cent., spelter being at the rate of £17 per ton in London, we should have :—

$100 - 30 = 70$ per cent.; and $40 - 1 = 39$ per cent.

$\frac{39 \times 100}{70} = 55\cdot 7$ per cent.; $55\cdot 7 - \frac{1}{5}(55\cdot 7) = 44\cdot 6$;

$44\cdot 6 - 1 = 43\cdot 6$;

$\frac{43\cdot 6 \times £16}{100} =$ . . . £6 19 0

Less return charges, . . 2 10 0

£4 9 6
Calcination loss at 30 per cent. of £4, 9s. 6d., 1 6 10

£3 2 8
Deduct cost of calcination, . . 0 5 0

Value per ton of crude calamine *ex*-ship at Swansea, dry weight, £2 17 8

Phosphate of lime is sold by the ton, the price obtained depending upon the percentage of phosphoric anhydride, which is determined by chemical analysis.

Mica is sold by the lb., the price increasing very rapidly with the size of the plates, and their freedom from wrinkles and flaws.

The ton, which so frequently forms the unit of weight by which minerals and metals are sold, varies in amount. The British statute ton contains 20 cwts., or 2,240 lbs.; the "long ton" has several values; 21 cwts. to the ton was, until very recently, generally employed in the sale of coal, but on account of altered railway rates it has almost gone out of use. In America the ton of 2,240 lbs. is employed under the name of the "long ton." The "short ton" of 2,000 lbs. is commonly used in the United States, Canada, and South Africa, while on the Continent the metric ton of 1,000 kilogrammes, equal to about 2,204 lbs., is used.

* For further information *re* ticketings, see Rickard's *Miners' Manual*, Truro, 1859.
† H. D. Hoskold, " Notes upon a practical method of ascertaining the value or price to be paid for zinc mineral." *Transactions of the Federated Institute of Mining Engineers*, vol. v., 1892-93, p. 93 ; also vol. vii., 1893-94, p. 228.

SALE OF PRODUCT.

Delivery of, and Payment for, Mineral.—Under this head we will consider one or two special cases, beginning with the simplest, illustrative of the methods employed.

Tin.—In Cornwall, the ore (*black tin*) having been bought by a certain firm at the ticketing, is sent to their works by horse and cart in bags each holding from 3 to 4 cwts. An officer of the Company accompanies the ore, and checks the weighing of it at the works. In addition to the deduction of 3 lbs. per cwt. already mentioned, the weight of each sack (3 to 4 lbs.) must be deducted, and then the net dry weight calculated. A receipt for the ore, showing the amount of money due, is then given to the representative of the Mining Company in the following or some similar form :—

TIN-BILL.

.... SMELTING HOUSE,
TRURO, *16th March, 1893.*

Messrs. .... *Mine Adventurers.*

BLACK TIN.

Tons.	Cwts.	Qrs.	Lbs.								
10	7	2	22	at £	57	0	0	per ton	£	591	18 8
				Carriage,	0	3	4	,,		1	14 7
									£	593	13 3

The item "carriage" requires some explanation. The Mining Company usually pays the carriage; when, however, ore is sold at a "ticketing" to works which are farther away than other works represented at the sale, it is evident, that because of the extra cost of carriage the Company might really be making less out of their ore, in spite of the price paid by the Company owning the distant works being greater than that offered by the nearer. To compensate the Mining Company in this matter, the smelter pays the excess of carriage beyond a certain distance.

Payment quickly follows the tin-bill either by cheque, or by a bill (see p. 84), payable in seven days, or in some other period up to two months. This latter is sometimes also known as a "tin-bill." *

The sales of tin are recorded in a book which may be ruled as follows :—

.... MINE, ..., 189

	TIN SOLD.				TIN SAMPLED.			
Date.	Pur-chasers.	Quantity.	Price per Ton.	Carriage. Date.	Tribute.	Tutwork.		Total.
					Tons. cwts. qrs. lbs.	Tons. cwts. qrs. lbs.		

The "tin sampled" is extracted from the sampling book (p. 22), and being entered in the right-hand page of the tin-sales' book, affords a check on the dressing of the ore.

Coal.—In the case of this mineral, the sales are so numerous that it is

---

* The old tin-bill was simply a promissory note to deliver a certain quantity of metallic tin to the miner at the next coinage. The coinages for tin were held four times a year at certain appointed towns, and no tin could go into the market until it had been stamped (see Pryce, *Mineralogia Cornubiensis.* London, 1778, p. 291).

necessary to employ several books. The original orders for coal and the contracts are kept at the office of the colliery, instructions as to the coal to be delivered being usually telephoned day by day to the weighman at his hut. Here the orders are written as received into the telephone-message book which thus becomes a sort of order-book. The orders are sometimes recorded in a more systematic order-book, as in the example given below :—

ORDERS RECEIVED.

Date.	No. of Order.	Ordered by	Address.	Consignee.	Address.	Quantity.	Quality.	Date Order Completed.

The actual orders are, of course, preserved, being either filed or pasted in a guard book.

Coal, as a rule, goes from the pit in railway waggons, and is weighed in them; but it sometimes goes by canal. In the Midlands, when sent by canal, it is not weighed before it is shot into the boats, the quantity being ascertained by gauging—that is, measuring the depth of immersion. As the weights corresponding to given draughts of each boat have been previously ascertained by experiment, it is easy to calculate the various boat-loads.

It is common to find a coal-yard attached to a colliery in order to supply local customers by means of carts. This is the "land sale" department.

In the case of railway traffic, the weight of each waggon, when empty (*tare*), must be ascertained. It is generally painted on the waggons, though not always correctly; hence the empty waggon is weighed as it goes past the weigh-hut to the pit, for the hut is always situated by the edge of the siding which connects the colliery with the main railway. When the waggons come back to the weigh-hut full, they are labelled by the weighman as to their destination, according to the instructions he has received. He then re-weighs them, and makes a record in a book sometimes called a **waggon-book**, sometimes a **consignment-book**, sometimes a **weigh-book**. The following is the form in use at a colliery in Lancashire :—

CONSIGNMENT-BOOK.

Date.	Consignee.	No. of Waggons.	Weight.			Quality.	Destination.
			Gross.	Tare.	Net.		

The following is another example,* with more detail :—

Date.	Destination.	Route.	Whom for.	On Whose Account.	Description of Coal.	Waggons.		Gross Weight.	Tare of Waggon.	Net Weight.	Charged Weight.	Invoiced.	Declared.	Posted.
						Owner.	No.							

* Gérard Van de Linde, *Lecture on Collieries*, London, 1888. Also published in *Accountant*, vol. xiv., London, 1888, pp. 287, 301, 319.

SALE OF PRODUCT. 51

The column under "charged weight" has reference to the 21 cwts. to the ton, spoken of on p. 48; and that under "posted" refers to the transaction being posted into the ledger, which will be better understood after reading Chapter X. The weighman also fills up a declaration giving particulars of the consignments to the railway company. The forms for this are often bound in a book with counterfoils; there may also be a form attached on which the railway company can acknowledge the receipt of the waggons. The following is an example:—

............................18...

* DECLARATION OF COAL, COKE, AND LIME TO BE FORWARDED BY THE MIDLAND RAILWAY COMPANY.

Carriage payable by the Grangetown Collieries, subject to the Rates and Conditions in force for the time being.

From	To	Route.	Consignee.	Ultimate Destination.	Description.	Waggons.		Weight.
						Owner.	No.	

An invoice or advice note is sent from the weigh-hut or office to the consignee. When nothing but an account of the numbers of the waggons and weight of coal in each waggon is sent, a post-card with a form printed on the back is useful.

It is important that waggons be not detained longer than necessary; for it is evident that the more journeys they make in a given time, the more profitable they are to the owners, who charge so much per ton hire for each journey. Sometimes the Colliery Company own the waggons, sometimes the Railway Company, and sometimes the Colliery Company may have them on hire from a waggon company. To keep a stricter watch on the movements of waggons, a waggon-book is often kept; it shows the date when each waggon left the mine, the place to which it was sent, and the date of return.

In the case of "land sales," the carts are weighed as they come into the yard empty, and as they leave it full. A ticket giving full particulars of coal delivered must always be handed to the customer. At one colliery the following statutory conditions † are printed on the back of each ticket:—

"Where coal is delivered by means of a vehicle, the seller must deliver or send by post or otherwise to the purchaser or his servant before any part of the coal is unloaded, a ticket or note in this form.

"Any seller of coal who delivers a less quantity than is stated in this ticket or note is liable to a fine.

"Any person attending on a vehicle used for the delivery of coal, who, having received a ticket or note for delivery to the purchaser, refuses or neglects to deliver it to the purchaser or his servant, is liable to a fine."

Five of these forms, one below the other, form a page of the "land sales-book." The right-hand portion is torn out and given to the customer, while the left-hand portion remains in the book, forming a permanent primary record.

At another colliery, tickets exactly like those described for the case of workmen on p. 24 are also used for general customers, and a book similar to that described on same page is used to make a summary of these sales for working up into the further accounts of sales, examples of which will be next described.

* Gérard Van de Linde, *op. cit.*
† *Vide* Weights and Measures Act, 1889 (52 and 53 Vict., c. 21), sec. 21.

At the colliery where the consignment-book mentioned above (p. 50) is used, the weighman makes up in his hut a subsidiary day-book, in which the total quantity of coal sent day by day to each consignee is recorded. It is ruled thus :—

WEIGH-HUT DAY-BOOK.

............................189...

Name.	Destination.	Quality.	No. of Waggons.	Coal.	Burgy.	Slack.

There are but three classes of coal sold at this colliery :—*Coal*, i.e., lumps from which the fine has been separated by screening ; *burgy*, i.e., unscreened coal ; and *slack*, or small coal which has fallen through the screen. In the column headed "quality" the name of the seam whence the coal came is entered. This book is sent to the office, and from it is made up the office day-book, which is similar in character. The sales' ledger is posted daily from the latter book (see p. 80), and monthly statements are made out from the ledger. The following is a further elaborated form of day-book :—*

Carriage Payable by.	Customer's Name.	Consignee (if necessary).	Station.	Owner of Waggon.	No. of Waggon.	Quality of Coal.	Gross Weight.	Tare.	Net at 20 cwts. per ton.	Net at 21 cwts. per ton.	Total Weight.	Coal Journal Folio.	Summary for Purposes of Cost Sheet.					
													Best Coal.		Nuts.		Slack.	
													Weight.	Price.	Amount.	Weight.	Price.	Amount.	Weight.	Price.	Amount.

From the day-book a **Coal Journal** is written up in which each customer has a page allotted to him.

COAL JOURNAL.†

JOHN SMITH, Coal Merchant, Peterboro'.

Date.	Best Coal, in Midland Waggons.	Nuts, in Midland Waggons.	Slack, in our Waggons.	Price.			Total Price.	Amount.	Total.	Ledger Folio.
				At Pit.	Carriage.	Waggon Hire.				

From this book, monthly statements are made out. The ledger is posted monthly also, but only with totals.

The monthly statements sent out to customers may either simply set down the total of each class of coal supplied and the money due, or they may set out the details of every consignment. Seeing that each consignment is checked, as it comes to hand, by means of the invoice, the total coal sent for

* R. J. Evans, "Lecture on Colliery Accounts." *The Accountant*, vol. xii., 1886, London, p. 56. See also the lecture by Mr. Gérard Van de Linde, above quoted.
† *Idem.*, p. 110.

SALE OF PRODUCT.

the month can readily be checked; it is consequently unnecessary to repeat the details in the monthly account, though in some cases it may save trouble.

The account may be made out in the form of an ordinary invoice. The following is a convenient form * when several kinds of coal are supplied to a merchant who may have several wharves; it can easily be modified to meet the actual requirements of any particular mine :—

GRANGETOWN, 1st Dec., 1887.

MR. RICHARD SMITH, Dr.,
 To THE GRANGETOWN COLLIERIES.

Terms.—Cash on the tenth of the following month and no discount allowed.

Cheques and Post-Office Orders to be made payable to the Grangetown Collieries or order.

Date.	To	Best Bright.					Trucks.	At	Amount.
		T. C.	T. C.	T. C.	T. C.		T. C.		£ s. d.
Dec. 1	Ilchester,	6 9					6 9	10/-	3 4 6

Silver Ores.—In Colorado the ore is often sent from the mine to a public sampler, trusted by seller and purchaser. The following is an example of the label used :—

.... MINE.

GUSTON, COLORADO.
......................189...

Lot No..
Car No.. Class of Ore...
Weight.. Extracted from.......................................
 Shipped to..
....

A daily report of ore shipments is made on the next form :—

GUSTON, COLO.,.............................189...

DAILY REPORT OF ORE SHIPMENTS.

From.................................... To..
....

Lot No.	Car No.	Classed as	Extracted from	Mine Weight.	Remarks.

Three samples are taken by the public sampler—one is sent to the seller, one to the purchaser, and one is retained. The sample sent to the mine is assayed there, or elsewhere, and the results entered in the assay-book :—

RECORDS OF ASSAY FOR..

Date	SAMPLE OR CONTROL.		ASSAY.						Remarks.
	Mark or Number.	Description.	Gold.	Silver.	Lead.	Copper.	Iron.	Silica.	

---

* Gérard Van de Linde, op. cit.

An account of the shipment, with composition of the ore, is now made out and forwarded to the smelting company purchasing it.

The Smelting Company also assays its sample and sends an account to the mine. If the two assays vary materially, and the difference cannot be amicably settled, recourse is had to the assay of the public sampler, who supplies the result of his analysis.

Of the three assays, the average of the two which most nearly agree is taken as the correct composition of the ore; when the result is agreed upon, a statement is forwarded by the Smelting Company to the mine, showing the amount of money due to the Mining Company on account of purchases. An example of such a statement is given herewith:—

Folio No..............

THE .... SMELTING

Bought of..

Assay No.	Lot No.	Cars.	Weights.			Assays.			
			Pounds Gross.	Per cent. Water.	Pounds Net.	Ounces Silver.	Per cent. Lead.	Ounces Gold.	Per cent. Copper (Dry).
	Silica, Iron, Mn., Zinc, Sulphur,								

New York Quotations. Date of Assay:—

Date	....	....	....	....
Silver	....	....	....	....
Lead	....	....	....	....
Copper	....	....	....	....

(*Continuation.*)

AND REFINING COMPANY.

(Date of Settlement.)

Denver, Colo., ...189......

Silver.	Lead.	Gold.	Copper.	Credit for Iron Excess.		Working Charges.		Price per Ton.		Gross Value.		Freight. at per ton.		Net Value.	
Percentage Paid.	Price per Unit.	Price per Ounce.	Price per Unit.	Dols.	Cts.	Dols.	Cts.	Dols.	Cts.	Dols.	Cts.	Dols.	Cts.	Dols.	Cts.

THE .... SMELTING AND REFINING COMPANY,

By..

SALE OF PRODUCT. 55

Following the statement, an account is sent by the Smelting Company, accompanied by a cheque or draft for the money due.

The carriage paid upon the ore (always by the Smelting Company) depends often upon its value; for the Railway Company may agree to take the poor ore for a smaller freight on condition that it is paid a larger freight on rich parcels. Hence it is necessary to send a "Certificate of Assay" to the Railway Company.

Finally, a complete record of each sale, and of all attendant circumstances, is written up in a long book, which is ruled as follows:—

STATEMENT OF ORES SHIPPED.   By.........................   ....

Date of Shipment.	Mine Lot No.	Car No.	Class of Ore.	How Shipped.	Extracted from	Mine Weight.	RAILROAD WEIGHT			Date of Sampling.	SAMPLING WORKS WEIGHT.				
							Gross.	Tare.	Net.		Gross.	Moisture.		Net.
												p. c.	Lbs.	

STATEMENT OF ORES SHIPPED—Continued.

ASSAY.				Sampling Charge.			Where Shipped.	BASIS OF SETTLEMENT.					
Au. Oz.	Ag. Oz.	Pb. p. c.	Cu. p. c.	Shipped in Car No.	Per Ton.	Total Amount.		Gold per Oz.	SILVER.		Lead per Unit.	Copper per Unit.	Cost of Treatment.
									Loss in Smelting.	N. Y. Quotations.			

STATEMENT OF ORES SHIPPED—Continued.

Amount per Ton Net.	Total Value of Ore.	DEDUCTIONS.			Date of Payment.	MINE CHECK SAMPLE.				REMARKS.
		Freight Paid.	Switching Charge.	Amount Received.		Assay.				
						Au.	Ag.	Pb.	Cu.	

Gold-Ore.—On the Rand the concentrates extracted from the pulp as it leaves the stamp-battery plates are in some cases packed into sacks and sold monthly to chlorination works. A representative of the Company accompanies them while they are being transported to the works. On arrival they are weighed and carefully sampled, three samples being taken. One of the samples is assayed by the Mining Company, another by the buyers, while the third is sealed up; should the assay of the seller differ from that of the buyer, the third sample is submitted to an independent assayer. Of the three assays, the mean of the two which most nearly agree is taken, in determining the amount of gold in the lot.

A record may be kept by the Mining Company in the following form :—

CONCENTRATES SOLD.

Return of..
Sold to...

WEIGHTS.

No. of Lot.	Net Wet Weight.	Percentage of Moisture.	Moisture Weight.	Net Dry Weight.	Net Weight in Tons of 2,000 Lbs.	
	Lbs.			Lbs.	Tons.	Lbs.

ASSAYING.

Lot Nos.	Ozs.	Dwts.	Grs.

Fine Gold.

SETTLEMENT.

Tons. Lbs. Ozs. Dwts. Grs.   Ozs. Dwts. Grs.
.... at .... per ton = ...
             Less.........per cent.,   .   .   .   = ...

                                                   At ...... per Oz.
                                                   £   :   :
      Less £   per ton for working charges, £   :   :
                                                   £   :   :

The above is an example of forms used where the concentrates are sold outright; in many cases, however, the chlorination works are under other agreements for working.

PART III.

WORKING SUMMARIES AND ANALYSES.

It would be possible to assign a great number of the books and forms used at mines to this Part, as they more or less partake of the nature of summaries and analyses; but some of them have already been described, and others, which constitute the most important part of a company's accounts, will be spoken of in the next Section. Here we shall more particularly consider those summaries and analyses which are of especial value to the manager of a mine. They show the totals of mineral gotten and dressed, the various costs of working and maintenance; by their help, comparisons can be made with previous periods, and costs can be compared with selling prices, and with costs at other works. The totals obtained are also useful for working up into the further accounts of a company.

Occasionally, statistical analyses of work-people employed, hours of labour, and wages are made, though this is comparatively rare.

We shall briefly consider at the end of this Part, the accounts sent home by a mine situated abroad.

It will be convenient to divide this Part into the following Chapters:—

Chapter VII.—Summaries of mineral raised, dressed, and sold; and of labour.
Chapter VIII.—Analyses of cost.
Chapter IX.—Forwarding accounts to head office.

CHAPTER VII.—SUMMARIES OF MINERAL RAISED, DRESSED, AND SOLD; AND OF LABOUR.

These summaries are usually made daily, and these, again, are further summarized weekly, fortnightly or monthly, as the case may be. The primary records from which they are compiled are generally used in connection with the payment of men, and several examples have been described under that head; one other example may be added, where the records are kept most carefully, though they are not required in calculating wages. At the De Beers Co.'s mines the following form, showing the amount drawn up each shaft every hour, is in use:—

DE BEERS CONSOLIDATED MINES, LD. (I). MORNING SHIFT.

Details of Blueground hauled per hour at................Shaft,................Mine,............189......

Hour.	16 Cubic Feet Loads per Hour.	Total.	Stoppages.									Remarks.
			Shaft.	Low Steam.	Bottom Haulage.	Top Haulage.			Boxes.		Winding Engine.	
						Haulage.	No Trucks.	No Ground.	Top.	Bottom.		
7-8												
8-9												
9-10												
10-11												
11-12												
12-1												
1-2												
2-3												
Bottom Tally, Top Tally,												Total Stoppages, ...hours....minutes.

....

                    Tallyman.   *Overman.*

These forms are bound in books with counterfoils, a white form being used for morning shift, green for afternoon, and pink for night.

The next is the daily return from the floors where the "blue ground" is deposited for weathering, and afterwards washed:—

DE BEERS CONSOLIDATED MINES, LD. (II).
DAILY FLOOR RETURN.

KIMBERLEY MINE,

..............................189......

BLUE DEPOSITED.		BLUE WASHED.			REMARKS.
		Machines.	Loads.	Carats.	
Day,		ROTARIES:			
Night,		Day, Night,			
		PULSATORS: Day, Night,			
Total,		Total,			
		FLOOR FINDS: ....Diamonds,			
		Total,			............Floor Manager.

SUMMARIES OF MINERAL AND LABOUR.

The next is a daily summary :—

DE BEERS CONSOLIDATED MINES, LD. (III).

HAULING.

	Morning.	Afternoon.	Night.	Total.	Loads Deposited.
Main Shaft,					On Section No.,
Standard Shaft,					,,
					,,
					,,
Total, . .					Total, . .

WASHING.

Machine No.	Section No.	Floor Loads.	Mine Loads.	Hard Blue Crushed.	Lumps Washed.	Lumps Deposited.	Hard Blue and Stones taken off.		
							Section.	Hard Blue.	Stones.
Total, . .									

KIMBERLEY MINE,..........................189......

While a monthly summary is made in the following form :—

DE BEERS CONSOLIDATED MINES, LD. (IV).

......................189......   ....189......

BLUE ON FLOORS.   BLUE ON FLOORS.
LUMPS ON FLOORS.   LUMPS ON FLOORS.
YIELD PER LOAD.   YIELD PER LOAD.

DE BEERS MINE,..........................189......

Date.	HAULING.				WASHING.							DIAMONDS FOUND.				
	Morning Shift.	Afternoon Shift.	Night Shift.	Total.	Floor Loads.	Mine Loads.	Lumps Washed.	Blue Washed.	Blue Crushed.	Lumps Crushed from Stocks.	Lumps Crushed direct from Cylinder.	Lumps Deposited.	In Mine.	On Floors.	Sand.*	"Wash-up."†	Total.
									No. 2 Crusher in red ink.	No. 2 Crusher in red ink.						

* Fine gravel picked dry by convicts.
† Ordinary process of dressing "blue ground."

MINE ACCOUNTS.

The returns for each day occupy a line, and weekly totals are obtained as well as monthly. In the upper left-hand corner a summary for the previous month is given.

At the Ferreira Gold Mine, the ore hoisted is recorded at the pit-top, the ore carried to the mill is noted by the transport overseer, and the amount received at the mill by the mill overseer; these three totals must agree. The record is made up day by day in the following form :—

I.—ORE SENT TO MILL.

Date.	No. 1 Main Shaft.	No. 2 Main Shaft.	Surface Deposit.	Total.	Total from South Reef.	Total from Main Reef.	Ore Deposited in Bins.	Ore left in Bins.	Ore Milled.	Remarks.
	Tons.	Tons.	Tons.	Tons.	Tons.	Tons.	Tons.	Tons.	Tons.	

The amount of amalgam and of gold obtained is recorded in great detail thus :—

II.

Date.	Am. from Inside Plates.	Am. from Outside Plates.	Am. from Box Stands.	Am. from Vanner Plates.	Am. from other Sources.	Total Am. Received.	Am. Retorted.	Weight of Retorted Gold.	Gold in Am.	Retorted Gold Smelted.	Loss in Smelting.
	Ozs.	Ozs.	Ozs.	Ozs.	Ozs.	Ozs.	Ozs.	Ozs.	Per cent.	Ozs.	Per cent.

II.—*Continued.*

Weight of Gold Bars.				BULLION ASSAYS MADE AT THE MINE.					Remarks.
				No. of Bar.	Fine Gold.	Fine Silver.	Average Assay.		
							Fine Gold.	Fine Silver.	
No.	ozs.	dwts.	grs.		in thousandths	in thousandths	in thousandths	in thousandths	

A summary of the work of the cyanide plant for treating tailings is made thus :—

SUMMARIES OF MINERAL AND LABOUR.

MacArthur-Forrest Recovery Plant.

Work-sheet for month ending .... 189......

Charge No.	Tanks.	Weight in Tons of 2,000 Lbs.	Assay per Ton of 2,000 Lbs.	Residues Assay per Ton of 2,000 Lbs.	Extraction per Ton of 2,000 Lbs.	Extraction on Charge.	Remarks.	Quantity of Solution Used.	Strength of Stock Solution.	Strength after Extraction.	Consumption per cent. on Ore.	Consumption per cent. on Ore.	Consumption Lbs. per Ton Ore.	Amount of Gold in Charge.	Percentage.

The concentrates are not treated on the mine, but are sold (p. 55). See also Chapter XIV. (p. 131) for a suggested scheme of analysis for a gold mine.

The following form for a daily summary of coal dealt with is used at a colliery in Lancashire :—

DAILY RETURN.

.............................189......   ....MINES.

RAISINGS.	Tons.	Cwt.	DISPOSAL.	Tons.	Cwt.
Stock this Morning, ...			Sales—H. Level, ...		
....			,, L. Level, ...		
....			Sundries, ...		
....			Cart Sales, ...		
....			Allowances, ...		
....			Locomotives, ...		
....			Brickfield, ...		
Surplus, ...			Fire Coal, ...		
....			Boilers, ...		
....			Underground Furnaces,		
....			Stocked To-day, ...		
....			Deficiency, ...		
....			Stock To-night, ...		

                                                                Tons.   Cwt.
Weighed To-day, ... Waggons,
Part loaded To-night, ...

Part loaded this Morning, ...

Consumption, ...

        * Gets, ...

A form of summary from a colliery in South Wales is next shown. It is made up every day—a horizontal line to a day—the vertical columns being totalled every week. Two pages suffice for a month, and so each opening of the book exhibits a daily, weekly, and monthly summary :—

* Total amount of coal raised for the day.

MINE ACCOUNTS.

No. 1 Pit.   LLANBRADACH COLLIERIES.   Little Rock Seam of House Coal.   DAILY OUTPUT.

Date 8....	Total Coal Raised as per Pit Top Machine.	Large.	Per cent.	Cobble.	Per cent.	Nut.	Per cent.	Pea.	Per cent.	Small.	Per cent.	Total sent for Sale.	Per cent.	Small for Boilers.	Smiths' and Colliery use.	Per cent.	Coal Sold to Workmen.	Per cent.	Local Sales at Colliery.	Per cent.	To Stock.	Loss.	Gain.	Total.

    Left-hand page.   *Right-hand page.*

It will be noticed that in this form there is a column for total coal raised as per pit-top machine; the columns for loss or gain are used according as to whether the coal accounted for is less or more than this respectively.

It is important that the quantity of coal consumed on a colliery should be carefully ascertained and recorded. To secure this result, it is best to make some-one responsible for this duty, and to employ printed forms.

The following forms * of daily returns are used at a colliery in Spain. They are of interest because at this colliery there is coal-washing plant and also briquette-making plant :—

RAW COAL RECEIVED AND DISTRIBUTED.

Received from the weigh-bridge, ...

Distribution.

To the Evrard washer, ...
To the Berard washer, ...
Sent away by rail, ...
Sold in Barruelo (land sales), ...

Consumption at Colliery
{
  Smithy, ...
  Lime-burning, ...
  Bárbara shaft, ...
  Evrard washer, ...
  Berard ,, ...
  Bouriez machine, ...
  Middleton ,, ...
  House-coal for employés, ...
  House-coal, various, ...
  Locomotive, ...
  Pumping engine of Bárbara shaft, ...
}
....

Total, .

BARRUELO,....................189......   *Foreman,*......................................

The following is the return from one of the washing machines :—

    Coal delivered to the Evrard washer, . . . }
              Previous stock, . . . } ....

Results obtained from the Washer.

For gas-making, Madrid, ...⎫
For general sale, ...⎬......................
....⎭

Slime deposited, ...
....
Shale, ...
Loss, ...
(Stock remaining), ...

Total, .

BARRUELO,......................189......   *Foreman,*......................................

---

* Oriol, *Contabilidad Minera*, 1894, Madrid, p. 60.

SUMMARIES OF MINERAL AND LABOUR.

The following is a return from one of the briquette-making machines :—

Middleton Briquette Machine.

Briquettes from Machine No. 1, ...
      ,,   ,,   No. 2, ...
Washed coal employed, ... ⎫
Pitch employed, ... ⎬ ....
                                 .... ⎭
    Output for the day, ...
      ,,   ,,   night, ...
BARRUELO,......................189......   *Foreman,*............................

The following is a form * for a daily or weekly summary from a colliery in the same neighbourhood:—

	RAW COAL			WASHED COAL						BRIQUETTES			COKE			SLIME		
	Quantity	Value	Amount	Quantity	Value	Amount	Quantity	Value	Amount	Quantity	Value	Amount	Quantity	Value	Amount	Quantity	Value	Amount
INGOINGS.†																		
Stock,																		
Received from the mine,																		
,, ,, washer,																		
,, ,, briquette machine,																		
,, ,, coke ovens,																		
....																		
Total Ingoings,																		
OUTGOINGS.																		
To the washer,																		
,, briquette machine,																		
,, coke ovens,																		
Total,																		
Sales—																		
Consumption on colliery,																		
....																		
Total Outgoings,																		
,, Ingoings,																		
Stock,																		

At a lead mine in Cumberland the following summary is made of quantities of ore raised and of concentrates sold :—

Month.	Ore Stuff sent to Dressing House.	Lead Ore sent to Market.	Per cent. of Total.	Blende sent to Market.	Per cent. of Total.	Iron Pyrites sent to Market.	Per cent. of Total.	Total.
January,								
February,								
March,								

* Oriol, *Op. cit.*, p. 77.   † To the coal-yard of the colliery.

On the back of the sheet containing the above is this analysis :—

MONTH.	LEAD ORE.						Similar Series of Columns for Blende and for Iron Pyrites come here.	CHARGES.			PROFIT AND LOSS.			OFFICE CHARGES.
	Quantity.	Assay.	Price per Ton.	Proceeds.	Royalty.	Net Proceeds.		Wages.	Stores.	Total Charges.	Total Net Proceeds.	Profit.	Loss.	
January, . February, . March, .														

It will be noticed that this form contains provision for costs of extraction and dressing, and for a statement of the profit and loss of working, so that part of it should, with strictness, be placed in the next chapter. A rigid classification, however, where forms vary so widely, is impossible.

In *Die Aufbereitung der Erze*,* Linkenbach gives the following scheme for a monthly summary of the results of dressing a lead-zinc ore. He also sets out schemes for each separate dressing process; for these the original work must be referred to :—

* *Berlin*, 1887, pp. 140-150.

SUMMARY.

Results of the Dressing of 1000 Kg. of Raw Ore, January, 1886.

		FINISHED PRODUCTS.									UNFINISHED PRODUCTS.			Deads and Tailings.	Dressing Cost.	
		Lead Ore.				Zinc Ore.					Rolls- & Stamps-Work.	Cobbing-smalls.	Total.			
		Nut Ore.	Pea Ore.	Sand Ore.	Slime Ore.	Total.	Nut Ore.	Pea Ore.	Sand Ore.	Slime Ore.	Total.					M. Pf.
		Kg.	Kg.	Kg.	Kg.	Kg.	Kg.	Kg.	Kg.	Kg.	Kg.	Kg.	Kg.	Kg.	Kg.	
1.	I. 300 kg. lump-ore, II. 666·66 kg. mine-smalls, III. 33·33 kg. deads costing in PRELIMINARY SEPARATION,	...	...	...	...	...	...	...	...	...	...	...	...	...	33·33	0 27·5
2.	From the above 300 kg. lump-ore in the COBBING,	34·22	...	...	...	34·22	13·20	...	...	...	13·20	170·74	10·73	181·47	71·11	0 84·3
3.	From the above 666·66 kg. mine-smalls, together with 10·73 kg. cobbing-smalls. Total, . 677·39 kg. in the MINE-SMALLS and COBBING - SMALLS DRESSING,	23·04	33·82	17·40	8·93	83·79	8·07	11·01	5·12	4·07	28·27	155·17	...	155·17	410·16	1 61·0
4.	From 325·91 kg. rolls- and stamps-ore yielded by the above process in the ROLLS- and STAMPS-WORK,	...	10·80	9·46	6·88	27·14	...	53·84	37·23	11·97	103·04	325·91	...	...	195·73	0 70·7
	Total, .	57·86	44·62	26·86	15·81	145·15	21·27	64·85	42·35	16·04	144·51	...	...	...	710·33	3 43·5

The dressed lead ore obtained during January contained on an average in 100 kg. 65·50 kg. lead and 56·10 g. silver, so that 1000 kg. of raw ore, dressed, is calculated to yield 95·07 kg. lead and 81·43 g. silver.

The dressed zinc ore obtained during January contained in 100 kg. 44·50 kg. zinc, so that 1000 kg. of raw ore, dressed is calculated to yield 64·31 kg. zinc.

MINE ACCOUNTS.

Labour Analyses.—These are important, especially for statistical purposes; but they are not often made. The following is an example :—

THE .... HÆMATITE STEEL CO., LD.
MINES DEPARTMENT.

Return of Workmen employed at.....................Mines............. Weeks ending...................189...

Fortnight Ending								
Days at work, . .								
Tons worked, . .								
MEN AND BOYS EMPLOYED. Under- ⎰ Miners, . ground ⎱ Labourers, . Aboveground, . .								
Total working Minerals, At other work, . .								
Total employed, . .								
SHIFTS WORKED PER MAN AND PER BOY. Under- ⎰ Miners, . ground ⎱ Labourers, . Aboveground, . .								
Total working Minerals, At other work, . .								
Total employed, . .								
TOTAL WAGES EARNED PER MAN AND PER BOY. Under- ⎰ Miners, . ground ⎱ Labourers, . Aboveground, . .								
Total working Minerals, At other work, . .								
Total employed, . .								
TOTAL TONS WORKED PER MAN AND BOY. Underground, . . Aboveground, . .								
Total working Minerals,								
TOTAL TONS WORKED PER MAN AND BOY PER SHIFT. Underground, . . Aboveground, . .								
Total working Minerals,								
AVERAGE EARNINGS PER MAN AND BOY PER SHIFT. Under- ⎰ Miners, . ground ⎱ Labourers, . Aboveground, . .								
Total working Minerals, At other work, . .								
Total employed, . .								

CHAPTER VIII.—ANALYSES OF COSTS.

ANALYSES of costs often give simply lump sums expended in different departments and for various kinds of work, but these should always be supplemented by costs worked out per ton of mineral gotten, or per unit of saleable product obtained; otherwise, their import is not so readily grasped. It is sometimes difficult to decide to what unit costs should be worked out: in the case of coal there is no difficulty—they are estimated per ton of coal accounted for—that is, the lump sums representing costs are divided by the weight of coal sold *plus* the weight of coal consumed on the mine; but in the case of gold-mining, should costs be worked out per ton of ore raised or per ounce of gold obtained? In the case of copper-mining, should they be worked out per ton of ore or per ton of metal; and, in the case of tin-mining, should they be calculated per ton of undressed ore (*tinstuff*), per ton of dressed ore (*black tin*), or per ton of metallic tin? In favour of working out costs per ton of crude ore it may be said that their amount depends, for the most part, on the amount of ore gotten—not strictly proportionately, for up to a certain point the cost per ton decreases with an increasing output—while the amount of gold, or copper, or tin in the ores would not, in many cases, influence the costs to any great extent. Pushing this idea further, the costs of preparatory and exploratory drivages, which are generally paid for by the yard or fathom, are sometimes calculated to one or other of these units, as the case may be. On the other hand, costs per unit of saleable product are very useful for comparison with selling prices; and thus it is that we find occasionally, on the same sheet, costs worked out per ton of crude ore and per unit of saleable product.

In comparing the costs at mines situated in different countries, it must clearly be remembered that mere figures showing the various costs per ton of ore are insufficient and may be very misleading; it is necessary, for a fair comparison, to know, in addition, the daily wages paid to workmen, hours of work, cost of materials and of carriage, the output, supply of water, and any other data which may affect the costs.

In any analysis it is evident that the necessary data must be fully and accurately recorded at the mine. For instance, it would be folly for a clerk in London to attempt to pick out from the pay-sheets of a mine in Australia the cost of getting ore and the cost of development work, unless these were very clearly distinguished on the sheets. In fact, where possible, it is better that analyses should be made at the mine.|

What is finally required in an analysis of costs is the total cost of mining the mineral and preparing it for the market. Various stages are passed through, and in each stage, the cost of treatment includes labour, stores, and possibly other expenses. An analysis may proceed in one of two ways—(1) a preliminary analysis of cost of labour, cost of stores, and other expenses may be made, and afterwards, a general analysis; or (2) the cost during each stage may be analysed direct, various heads being adopted, and under each head a subdivision into cost of labour, stores, and other expenses may be made. Analyses of the cost of particular work are sometimes useful.

First Method.—The De Beers analyses of costs form a good example of the first method. The wages are analysed thus:—

MINE WAGES.

No. of Account.	Account.	European.	Native.		Totals.
	Hauling—				
	Breaking and Filling,				
	Tramming,				
	Hoisting, Rock Shaft,				
	,, West-end Shaft,				
	,, No. 1 Shaft,				
	General Repairs,				
	Shaft Repairs,				
	Dead Work,				
	Sundry Mine Expenses,				
	Pumping,				
	Mechanical Haulage,				
	Depositing,				
	Percentages,				
	Standing Charges,				
	Washing—				
	Harrowing,				
	Watering,				
	Loading,				
	Tramming,				
	No. 1 Machine,				
	,, 2 ,,				
	,, 8 & 9 ,,				
	Lumps,				
	Crushing Lumps,				
	Hard Blue,				
	Crushing Hard Blue,				
	Stones,				
	Cleaning Floors,				
	Percentages,				
	Superintending,				
	Sundry Floor Expenses,				
	Sinking Shafts—				
	Rock Shaft,				
	West-end Shaft,				
	No. 1 Shaft,				
	Compounds—				
	Stable,				
	West end,				
	Machinery, Plant, &c.,				
	Departments—				
	Electrical Department,				
	Stables,				
	Convict Labour,				
	Locomotives,				
	Pulsator,				
	Water (Dam),				
	Water (Wells),				
	Sundry Charges,				

GENERAL WAGES.

No. of Account.	Account.	European.	Native.		Totals.
	Stores Department— Firewood Depot, Coal ,, Removing Machinery,				
	Workshop Expenses— Foundry, Workshop Compound,				
	Workshop Plant— Carpenters' Shop, Machine, Foundry, Truck Repairers' Shop,				
	Kenilworth— Estate Charges, ,, Improvements, Village Extension, ,, Charges,				
	Farm Properties— Sundry Expenses, Fencing, Plant and Improvements,				
	Head-Office Charges— Stockdale Street Stables, Maintenance of Property, General Charges,				

In the analysis of stores, the columns are as follows, the accounts involved being exactly the same as those given in the preceding form of analysis of wages:—

No. of A/c.	Account.	Sundries.	Oils and Grease.	Paraffin & Candles.	Timber, &c.	Totals.
	Hauling— Breaking and Filling, Tramming, Hoisting, Rock Shaft, ,, West End ,, ,, No. 1 Shaft, &c., &c., &c.					

Preparatory to filling up this analysis, the following form is used for collecting the various items for each account, so as to obtain the totals required.

	ACCOUNT No.				ACCOUNT No.			
Order No.	Sundries.	Oils and Grease.	Paraffin & Candles.	Timber,&c.	Order No.	Sundries.	Oils and Grease.	Paraffin & Candles.	Timber,&c.

Finally, there are general analyses of the total cost of hauling and of washing blue ground. The "hauling" analysis is herewith given, that for "washing" being similar in character.

COST OF HAULING BLUE GROUND AT DE BEERS MINE

	Breaking and Filling.	Underground Tramming.	HOISTING.		General Repairs.	Shaft Repairs.	Dead Work.
			Rock Shaft.	West End Shaft.			
Labour. Contractors,							
Salaries,							
Wages. White,							
,, Native,							
Convict Labour,							
Repairs. Mechanics. White,							
,, Native,							
Workshops,							
Stores. Timber,							
Paraffin and Candles,							
Oils and Grease,							
Sundries,							
Fuel. English Coal,							
Colonial Coal,							
Wood,							
Water,							
Stables,							
Locomotives,							
Electric Lighting and Power,							
Sundries,							
Loads Hauled,							
Average Cost per load,							

The following is a form for a much simpler analysis of wages. It will be noticed that the cost during the previous month is given; this is very useful for comparison:—

Cost.	Cost per ton last month.	Cost per ton this month.	Amount.
Wages.—Miners for Raising Ore, &c.,			
,, ,, Fathom Work,			
Trials,			
Underground Labourers and Captains, &c.,			
Mechanics,			
Loco-Men, Engine-Men, & Cleaners,			
Browmen, Pickers, Trimmers, &c.,			
Platelayers, Labourers, &c.,			
Clerks and Surveyors,			
Total Wages,			

ANALYSES OF COSTS.

for .... *weeks, from* .... *to* .... , *inclusive.*

Sundry Mine Expenses.	Pumping.	Mechanical Haulage.	Depositing.	Percentages.	Standing Charges.	Totals.

At Llanbradach a very complete weekly analysis of all materials used is made in the following form:—

Material.	Quantity.	At	Amount.	Total.
Pitwood,				
Cogwood,				
Coal consumed—Large,				
„ Small,				
Sleepers,				
Rails—Bridge,				
„ Flange,				
„ Heavy,				
Fish Plates,				
„ Bolts,				
&c., &c., &c.				

At the end, there is space for making a separate list of all material used for new work, which goes to capital account.

A briefer analysis of stores and miscellaneous expenses is also made thus:—

MINE ACCOUNTS.

Stores, Royalties, Taxes, &c.						Cost per Ton.	
	T.	C.	£	s.	d.	s.	d.
Boiler Coal,							
Winding and Guide Ropes,							
Hauling Ropes,							
Rails and Sleepers,							
Iron and Steel,							
Timber,							
Oil and Grease,							
General Stores,							
Electrical Goods,							
Repairs and Renewals,							
Royalties,							
Taxes,							
Incidentals, Rent,							
Telephone, &c.,							
Total,							

At a gold mine on the Rand, the following analyses of costs are made each month.

First, there is a series of preliminary analyses, the principal being:—

"Compound" costs.
Hoisting and Pumping costs.
Tramming costs.
Smith's costs.
Rock-Drill costs.
Compressor costs.
General charges.

The compound costs are necessarily made up first, so that the cost per native may be ascertained for use in making up other costs. The form used is as follows:—

COMPOUND COST.

	Amount.	Working Place.	No. Boys.	Cost per Boy.	Amount.
Wages—Europeans.		Stopes,	500		
,, Natives, Policemen,		Drift 900 East,	10		
Materials—		,, 900 West,	5		
Meat,		Cross Cut 1120,	4		
Meal,		Drift 620,	10		
Salt,		,, 720,	20		
Water,		,, 820,	30		
Sanitary,		,, 520,	40		
Fuel—		Mill,	16		
Wood,		Cyanide,	50		
Coal,		Sorting,	25		
		&c., &c.			
Total cost,		Total No. Boys,			

On the left hand is set out the cost, and on the right the number of boys * working in the various places, the cost per boy, and the proportionate amount of cost which goes against each working place for keep.

Hauling and pumping costs are set out in a very similar manner.

* "Boy" = native workman of any age.

HAULING AND PUMPING COSTS.

	Amount.	Working Places.	Tons Rock Broken.	@ per Ton	Cost of each Working Place.
Wages—		1120 Cross Drift,	240		
Engine-Drivers,		920 Drift E shaft,	175		
Overtime,		920 ,, W ,,			
Natives,		820 ,, E ,,			
,, Keep,		820 ,, W ,,			
,, Overtime,		&c.			
Materials—		&c.			
Oils,		Stopes,	8,000		
Waste,					
Fuel—					
Tons Coal, @					
		Total No. of tons,			

It will be noticed that in this case the cost is worked out per ton broken, and that the total cost is distributed to the various places in proportion to the number of tons broken. To determine the number of tons broken, the cubic content of each excavation, in feet, is divided by 13—*i.e.*, 13 cubic feet to the ton.

The costs in the other cases of this series are ascertained and distributed in an exactly similar manner, except "general charges." In this analysis the mine and the mill are each charged half of the wages of the engineer, assayer, timekeepers, storemen, buyers, and others who divide their time between the mine and the mill. The portion of general charges allotted to the mine is further distributed to each working place in proportion to the amount of stone broken.

The second series of analyses consists of:—
> Capital account,
> Development account,
> Stoping account,
> Sorting account,
> Milling account.

Work done in shafts is charged to capital account, while drifts, cross-cuts, and winzes go into development account. These two accounts are exactly similar in character; they are made up from pay-sheets, store-books, steel-book, and the first series of analyses already described. The following form shews the manner in which they are arranged:—

DEVELOPMENT ACCOUNT ....189...

Situation.	Progress for Month. Feet.	Price per Foot.	WAGES.			Explosives.	Materials.	Hauling and Pumping.	Tramming.	General Charges.	Smiths' Cost.	Steel Used.	Rock Drill Cost.	Compressor Cost.	Totals.	Cost per Foot.
			Europeans.	Natives, and Keep.												

..........Tons Developed Reckoning Milling width of Reef .... feet ⎫
..........Tons Developed Reckoning Mining width of Reef .... feet ⎬ Average cost per foot ....

The cost in the above analysis is worked out per foot of ground driven. The stoping account is very similar, except that the places from which the rock comes are not specified. The cost is worked out per ton of rock raised and per ton of reef raised.

The milling account is in the following form; cost being worked out per ton milled :—

| Running Time. | | WAGES. | | Materials. | Fuel. | General Charges. | Totals. | Cost per Ton |
Days.	Tons Milled.	Europeans.	Natives, and Keep.					

A third series of three analyses is afterwards made in a book, called "**Mine Cost and Value Book.**" They are made under the heads :—

> Winzes and Rises.
> Cross Drifts.
> Drifts in Reef.

Part of the data they contain is extracted from the development account. The following example will illustrate their character :—

MINE COST AND VALUE BOOK.

Winzes and Rises.

Month	Year.	Winze or Rise.	Ft. Feet Done. Ins.	Cost Sinking or Rising.	Incidental Cost.		Total Cost.	Cost per Foot.	Width of Reef.	Total Tons Extracted.	Tons of Reef Extracted.	VALUE PER TON.						Value of Reef Extracted.
					Particulars.	Amt.						Amalgamation Assay.			Fusion Assay.			
				£ s. d.		£ s. d.	£ s. d.	£ s. d.				ozs	dwt.	grs.	ozs.	dwt.	grs.	£ s. d.

Second Method.—The analyses made at the Barruelo Colliery * in Spain will serve as an example of this method. The first classification is under the heads :—

> Extraction of coal, { General costs.
> { Costs of extraction.
> Washing coal.
> Briquette manufacture.
> Coke manufacture.

Under each of these heads there are many subdivisions. The following form for the costs of briquette manufacture will illustrate the method of ruling and give some idea of the method of subdivision employed. It will be noticed that the various items and totals are entered for the current month, and also for the previous month; the costs per ton are also treated similarly :—

* Oriol, *Op. cit.*, p. 79.

ANALYSES OF COSTS.

MANUFACTURE OF BRIQUETTES.	Current Month.		Previous Month.		Totals.		AVERAGE PER TON.		
							Current Month.	Previous Month.	Total.
	Items.	Total.	Items.	Total.	Items.	Total.			
COST OF MANUFACTURE.									
1. *Supervision.*									
i. Fixed salary,									
2. *Labour.*									
i. Day workers,									
3. *Working Machines.*									
i. Labour,									
ii. Raw coal,									
iii. Slimes,									
4. *Transport.*									
i. Labour,									
ii. Materials,									
iii. Traction,									
iv. Loading waggons,									
5. *Various Costs.*									
i. Lighting,									
6. *Upkeep of Machines.*									
i. Labour,									
ii. Materials,									
iii. Oiling,									
7. *Upkeep of Buildings.*									
i. Labour,									
ii. Materials,									
iii. Sundries,									
8. *Upkeep of Tools.*									
i. Labour,									
ii. Materials,									
9. *Binding Materials.*									
i. Pitch,									
ii. Tar,									
Total cost of manufacture,									
COMBUSTIBLES.									
Raw coal,									
Washed coal,									
Slime,									
Total cost,									

Another good example of this method is given by Ludlow in the *Engineering and Mining Journal*, vol. lii., p. 566.

When analyses are in great detail several sheets may be used in making them. Sometimes, however, on a single sheet there is a summary of all mineral raised, dressed, and sold, and analyses of costs, showing at a glance the result of working for the period considered. When mines are at a distance from the Head Office some such compact general summary should be sent to the directors.

It is advantageous to arrange that the weekly, monthly, and yearly* analyses shall be of the same character, so that the data collected for the weekly analysis shall be available for the monthly one, and those of the latter for the yearly analysis.

The actual working out of costs is a very trying task; it is much facilitated by the use of calculating machines or slide-rules. Mr. Emerson Bainbridge has designed a special slide-rule for calculating mine costs.

The student will find further examples of analyses in Chapter XIV., and in the books and articles mentioned below.

> Carter, Practical Book-keeping, 6th ed., Edinburgh, 1890, pp. 72, 73, and 74, and folding sheets: No. vi., A, B, C, D and E.
> Oriol, Contabilidad Minera, Madrid, 1894 (many good examples).
> Evans, "Colliery Accounts" (lecture), *The Accountant*, vol. xii., London, 1886, pp. 57 and 58.
> Van de Linde, "Collieries" (lecture), *The Accountant*, vol. xiv., London, 1888, pp. 325 and 326.
> Carey, "Colliery Cost Sheets," *Trans. National Association of Colliery Managers*, vol. v., London, 1893, p. 99.
> James, "Collieries" (lecture), *Trans. Chartered Accountants' Students' Society of London*, 1894, p. 154.
> Prest, "Colliery Cost Sheets," *Trans. Federated Institution of Mining Engineers*, vol. ix., 1894-95, pp. 239-242.
> Bulman and Redmayne, Colliery Working and Management, London, 1896, ch. vii.

CHAPTER IX.—ACCOUNTS FORWARDED TO HEAD OFFICE.

FREQUENTLY the head office of a mining company is situated a long way from the mine, in which case the manager is generally required to send, for the satisfaction of the directors and auditors of the company, a monthly report of the condition and prospects of the mine, accounts of all transactions, and sometimes an estimate of the financial requirements of the undertaking for the ensuing month.

For the accounts, it is usual to employ forms similar to some of those which have already been described. The currency is naturally that of the country in which the mine is situated; "translation" to English or other money, as the case may be, being done in the home-country. Information on the following points is usually sent :—

1. Salaries and wages paid.
2. Purchases, consumption, and stock of stores.
3. Sales of product.
4. Cash account.
5. Ore raised and treated.

The character of the accounts forwarded varies very much; sometimes the accounts are in full detail, and accompanied by vouchers for every item of expenditure; at other times they are simply summaries, and are accompanied

* See Chapter XIV.

by no vouchers whatever ; in the latter case there is a local audit, or, more rarely, the manager on the spot checks every item and signs the accounts.

CASE A.—As an example of the first case, may be mentioned the usage of a mine in Colorado, worked by a London company.

Salaries and Wages Paid.—Complete copies of the pay-sheets are sent, with receipts, one signed by each man who has received pay. These receipts are signed in duplicate, one being retained at the mine, and the other sent to London.

Guston, Colorado,...*189*......

No............ *Name*.................................... *Occupation*...................................

Received from THE..COMPANY, Limited.

....*Dollars*,

in full payment for services for the month ending........................*189*......

........*Days,* @ $...................... . . . . $......................

Deductions :—Insurance, . . $......................
   Board, ...

....

   Amount due, ... $......................

.... *Signature*......................................

Purchases, Consumption, and Stock of Stores.—Each merchant's account is triplicated, and the three which are sent with the cheque in payment are receipted. One is retained at the mine, and the two others are forwarded, at different dates, to London. Thus, should one be lost, there is a probability of the other reaching its destination in safety. An account of the stock of stores, timber, and coal at the beginning of the month ; of the purchases and consumption during the month, and of stocks at the end of the month is also forwarded.

Sales of Product.—The statements (see p. 54) sent by the smelting companies are in duplicate, and one of each pair is sent to London.

Cash Account.—A cash statement showing only totals of wages paid, but full details of every other payment and of each item of income, is forwarded on a form headed "Cash Statement."

On the left is a column for the date, then comes a space for items, and finally there are two cash columns ; the first being for all amounts received and the other for payments. When the total of the first column exceeds the total of the second, the difference is "cash in hand."

Ore Raised and Treated.—The ore is an argentiferous copper ore carrying a considerable percentage of copper ; it is not dressed to any extent, but is sold direct to smelting companies. A copy of the detailed account of ore shipped, similar in character to that described on p. 55, is forwarded ; and also an account of any ore in stock.

CASE B.—The example given below will illustrate the case where vouchers are not forwarded. The following statements are sent from a gold mine on the Continent to its head office in London.

Salaries and Wages.—An abstract of the pay-sheet is sent showing the number of men and total wages for each class of work where the men are paid by the day, but in the case of the miners who work on contract the earnings of each company are shown. There is also a sheet sent showing the bargains which have been let to the men for the ensuing month.

Purchases and Stock of Stores.—A summary under several heads of stock at beginning of month, of purchases during month, and of stock at end of month is forwarded.

Sales.—The gold is sold through an agent resident at a large town in the district, so that there is an account of gold forwarded to him from the mine, and an account from him of the value of the gold, with amount of deductions for assays, &c.

Cash Account.—A copy of the "Cash Account" from the mine ledger (see next part) is made and forwarded.

Ore Raised and Treated.—An account is sent which shows amount and value of ore in stock at beginning of month, raisings for the month, and stock at end of month. There is also a complete monthly amalgamation account, similar to that described on p. 60; besides which a briefer amalgamation account is forwarded every week.

In many cases a well-designed, if not very elaborate, analysis of costs would greatly enhance the value of accounts sent home from mines abroad. For although sufficient data for the making of such an analysis may be included in the information sent, yet the draughting of it by a clerk who has little conception of what a mine is like, and who cannot be overlooked in his work by the mine-manager, is scarcely likely to lead to either useful or reliable results. These analyses should show clearly the cost of each class of work, and also what cost appertains to development and prospecting, and what to working expenses properly so called. Numerous examples of analyses have already been given.

PART IV.

CHAPTER X.—HEAD OFFICE BOOKS.

THE books which will be considered in this chapter contain the permanent records of transactions in a concise form for future reference, and also serve as the basis from which the "Revenue" or "Profit and Loss" Accounts are prepared at the balancing periods.

The summaries and analyses of transactions have been fully described in previous chapters, and information has been given as to the best form of supplying details to the Head Office, and we have now to consider what further records it is necessary to keep.

The chief book in the accounts of a business concern is the **Ledger** (*Hauptbuch*, Ger.; *Grand livre*, Fr.). All other accounts are subordinate thereto and lead up to it, the main object of preliminary records being to relieve the ledger of masses of detail. In addition to the books already described which relieve the Ledger of detail, there are others—principally the **Cash Book**, two **Bill Books**, and the **Journal**, devoted more or less to the same purpose, though the latter does not invariably contain more detail than the Ledger. These four books have a further important function. It must be clearly understood that the Ledger is a book of the very first importance; hence, it is desirable that alterations in it should never be necessary. With this object in view the entries for the Ledger are arranged in order in the Journal, Cash Book, and Bill Books, so that the Ledger can be posted from them with the least likelihood of error. It is, however, impossible but that errors will occur, in which case *there should be no erasing;* the faulty entry should be ruled through, and the correction written above.

The detailed accounts of the relations of a company with its shareholders are contained in the **Share Register** and **Dividend or Call Books**.

In the ledger the various transactions are arranged under headings written at the top of the pages (see example at end of chapter). Each set of entries under a heading is an *account;* the accounts being *personal* or *real,* according as to whether they are opened to persons or things, or *nominal,* if they do not relate directly to either persons or things, but are necessary in order to exhibit clearly the financial position of a business. The twofold character of every transaction is recorded by entering (*posting*) it twice—on the debtor side of one account and on the creditor side of another account.

The use of the words "debtor and creditor" is often very confusing at first to the student, who finds a difficulty in deciding whether an item should go to the debit or credit side of an account. Perhaps the following simple mnemonic aid may be of some slight help. We will suppose him seated before the open Ledger ready to post a transaction to a particular account; as an official he would, of course, represent the mining company; then, if he has any doubt as to which side of the account the item should go, let him imagine the heading personified, and saying to him—

> Debit what I got, credit what I gave ;
> So will you your own credit save.

The meaning of the "to" prefixed to the item on the debtor side of the account, and of the "by" on the creditor side, will now be clear. For example, a Drysalter supplying Oil is debtor *to* cash and creditor *by* oil. These particles are generally used in this country, but in America they are sometimes dropped.

An important point in posting the Ledger is to isolate each transaction, and to consider whether it goes to the debit or credit side of an account purely on its own merit without reference to any other transactions. Thus, although for the continuance of the ordinary relations of life, buying an article and paying for it are two transactions intimately connected with each other, yet, in posting one transaction into a Ledger, the existence of the other must be ignored. After the items have been correctly posted, the Ledger shews clearly the relation of the various transactions to each other.

The pages of the Ledger are not used consecutively, but the accounts are scattered through all parts of the book, each opening being numbered, and an index of the accounts made to facilitate reference.

Notwithstanding the fact that much detail is kept out of the ledger, still, in large undertakings, it often consists of several books, each of which contains a certain class, or certain classes, of transactions. In this case, however, there is usually a smaller book, called a **General Ledger** or **Private Ledger,** which contains a summary of the larger ledger, as well as a few accounts which the larger ledger does not include ; thus, it is in this smaller ledger only that a *complete* account of the financial position of the concern is contained.

In the case of a mining company when two volumes are used, one may be a General Ledger and the other a Private Ledger, or one may contain all personal accounts and the other the real and nominal accounts. At a colliery in Lancashire the following volumes are used :—First, there is a **Materials Ledger** ; this contains chiefly real accounts of stores, &c., bought, arranged under a number of heads (see p. 44), but it also includes accounts of royalty paid, of trespass rents, of wages, &c.—in short, it comprises accounts of the various items of expenditure which must be set against the value of the coal gotten. Secondly, corresponding to this, there is a ledger which contains personal accounts only. It is called a **Purchase Ledger,** or **Bought Ledger.** Thirdly, there is the **Sales Ledger,** with only personal accounts of coal sold. Finally, there is a **Private Ledger.** In the case of very large concerns, a still greater number of ledgers may be requisite.

Principal Accounts of a Mining Company.—The principal accounts met with in the ledgers of Mining Companies are the following :—

Personal Accounts, including those of Merchants, or other persons, from whom purchases have been made ; and of Merchants or Smelters, to whom products have been sold.

Real Accounts, comprising Mines or Claims, Land, Shafts and other Permanent Work, Machinery and Plant, Buildings, Cottages, Barracks or Compounds, Waggons (c), Live Stock, Furniture, Investments, Cash, Bills Receivable, Bills Payable, Stores (generally three or more accounts), Stationery, and Products of Mine.

Nominal Accounts, embracing Capital, Application, Allotment, Instalments, Calls, Dividends, Purchase, Sales, Discount and Interest, Waggon Hire (c), Cottage Rents, Land Sales (c), Interest on Investments, Wages, Salaries,

HEAD OFFICE BOOKS. 81

Directors' Fees, Auditors' Fees, Rates and Taxes, Royalty Rents, Railway Rates (Carriage of product), Insurance, General Charges, Bad Debts, Reserve Fund, Working Account (one or several), and Profit and Loss Account.

Note.—The accounts followed by (c) pertain more particularly to Colliery Accounts.

The following classification of the above accounts may be of some help to the student :—

Capital Accounts.
{ Capital—Application, Allotment, Instalments, Calls.
  Accounts connected with Capital Expenditure.
  { Purchase.
    Mines or Claims.
    Property (land, &c.).
    Shafts and other Permanent Work.
    Machinery, Plant, and Tools.
    Buildings.
    Cottages, Barracks or Compounds.
    Waggons (c).
    Live Stock.
    Furniture.
    Investments.
  }
}

Accounts connected with current Receipt and Expenditure.
{ Accounts connected with Expenditure.
  { Personal Accounts.
    Bills Payable.
    Stores (3 or several accounts).
    Stationery.
    Salaries.
    Wages.
    Directors' Fees.
    Auditors' Fees.
    Rates and Taxes.
    Royalty Rents.
    Railway Rates.
    Insurance.
    General Charges.
  }
  Accounts connected with Expenditure and Income.
  { Cash.
    Discount and Interest.
  }
  Accounts connected with Income.
  { Personal Accounts.
    Bills Receivable.
    Land Sales (c).
    Waggon Hire (c).
    Cottage Rents.
    Product.
    Interest from Investments.
  }
}

Working Accounts (1 or several).
Profit and Loss Account.
Dividends.
Reserve Fund.
Bad Debts.

The accounts opened in any particular case depend entirely upon the character of the transactions, and, therefore, upon the character of the mine, and upon the way in which its business is arranged; the variations met with are, consequently, considerable. Brief explanations will now be given of such of the more important accounts as seem to require them. The example at the end of the Chapter should be studied by the student in connection with these explanations.

Capital Account.—Suppose that a man, on starting business, has a certain sum of money which is spent in providing plant, or in development. This money must be accounted for in his books; and, as an individual cannot be debtor or creditor to himself, he opens a nominal account, which he calls "Capital Account." If there are two or three partners in a business, there are two or three capital accounts, one for each partner. Should a profit result from a year's work, and be left in the business, in some cases capital account would be credited with it, and the new capital for starting another year would be so much the greater. Should loss result, then the capital account would be debited with this loss, and the capital for starting the new year would be less. It is most usual nowadays, however, for a considerable number of partners to have an interest in a mining concern, the amount of the interest of each being expressed by their holding a certain number of shares of definite nominal value. The capital in this case is the total number of shares issued multiplied by the nominal value of a single share, and the amount does not increase or decrease with profit or loss, or with increased or decreased value of the mine, but is a fixed amount. Only the total capital, with particulars of the number and value of the shares, goes into the ledger; the details of shares held by different individuals being contained in the "**Share Register**" or "**Share Ledger**," which may most conveniently be described in the Chapter on "Companies'" books.

Sales and Purchase Accounts.—If a part of the property of a Company be sold, the money received must be looked upon as returned capital, not current income; hence a separate account, "**Sales Account**," is opened to receive the record of such sale. Again, if a mine be purchased by a Company, a "**Purchase Account**" would be opened to record it (see example at end of Chapter). The purchase account belongs to the next class, properly speaking.

Capital Expenditure Accounts.—The accounts are debited with all expenditure which results in the acquirement of something of permanent value to the mine owners. Such expenditure is most common during the early life of a mine, when the capital is being spent in purchasing the property, developing the mine, and equipping it with plant and machinery; but items are debited to capital expenditure accounts more or less during the greater part of the life of the mine: they may also be credited with sums taken out of income for depreciation year by year (see p. 109), though the more usual course is to credit such depreciations to a special reserve account. The accounts may be few or many, depending to some extent on the character of the transactions, but also on the method of classification adopted, as shown in the following three examples:—

Colliery outlay.	Claims.	Claims.
Cottage outlay.	Farms and landed property.	Machinery, plant, and tools.
Waggon outlay.	Shafts, &c.	
	Machinery and plant.	Permanent works.
	Offices and compounds.	Buildings.
	Office furniture.	Permanent water-works.
	Investments.	Live stock, carts, &c.
		Furniture.

Examples of other methods of classifying these accounts will be found by referring to the balance sheets of Mining Companies where these accounts are invariably published.

It is often a somewhat delicate matter to decide what expenditure should be set down as "Capital Expenditure," and what as "Current" or "Revenue Expenditure," for it is evident that if in any year a considerable part of the expenditure is written down against capital, then the current expenses will appear less, and the profit correspondingly greater; while if, on the other hand, the cost of what is of permanent value is charged against the current expense of one year, a true profit, in respect to ordinary working expenses and receipts, may be turned into an apparent loss.

If depreciation is written off at a liberal rate, the ill effect of over-charging capital accounts is neutralised to some extent; but it is better to charge as much as possible to current expenses accounts. Reference will be made to this matter in the next Chapter.

Personal Accounts.—An account is opened with each of the merchants from whom purchases are made, except in the case of very small items, which are entered into a Petty Cash Book (see p. 84); and there is also an account with each merchant, consumer, or smelter, to whom the product is sold, but detailed accounts are not opened to show the numerous small transactions connected with land sales at collieries. These accounts, being numerous, are usually entered in a Trade Ledger.

Stores Accounts.—These are debited with goods and materials purchased. There may be a single account, or there may be several. Here are three examples:—

1. (*Subdivision often used*).	2. (*In use at a Colliery*).	3. (*In use at a Hæmatite Mine*).
General Stores.	Candles and Powder.	General Stores.
Timber.	Cloth.	Iron.
Coal.	Fuel.	Oil and Grease.
	Iron.	Coal.
	Iron Castings.	Timber.
	Lamps and Wicks.	
	Lime and Cement.	
	Nails and Bolts.	
	Oil and Grease.	
	Pit Boxes (waggons).	
	Pit rails.	
	Provender.	
	Ropes and Cord.	
	Saddlery.	
	Timber and Props.	
	Tools.	
	Sundries.	
	Carriage (in stores).	

Wages Account.—It would be well-nigh impossible to open a personal account with every workman, and it is unnecessary, as every detail connected with money paid to workmen is recorded on the pay-sheets. Hence, it is only essential to credit the Cash Account with the total wages every "pay," and to debit a "Wages" Account with the same sum.

Either the total wages after stores have been deducted, or the gross wages before stores have been deducted, may be posted in this account. In the latter case, the amount deducted for stores may be credited to "Stores" Account or to a separate account called "Miners' Stores" Account. Perhaps the first method is the better—*i.e.*, not to allow the deductions for stores to go into the ledger at all; for whatever may be the arrangement in detail, the ultimate result is that the cost of stores goes against the mine, and it is better that it should appear under "Stores" than under "Wages."

Bad Debts Account.—When money owing to a company cannot be recovered, it is of no use to retain the amount in the ledger as an asset—that is, debited to some personal account; therefore the account is balanced by crediting it "By Bad Debts," and the "Bad Debts" Account is debited with the amount. When closing the books for the preparation of the balance sheet, the total bad debts are written off to Profit and Loss Account.

Cash Account.—The entries in the Cash Account are very numerous, because it receives the record of transactions which in their reverse aspect are distributed over many accounts—chiefly personal. For this reason this amount is kept in a separate **Cash Book**. The Cash Book may be ruled exactly like the Ledger; but a tabular form, with columns for recording discount and interest, and more or less analytical in character, is frequently used. An example of a Cash Book is here given:—

MINE ACCOUNTS.

Dr. *Cr.*

Date.	Name.	Ledger Folio.	Railway Bank.	Yard.	Agency.	Discount.	Cash.	Date.	Name.	Ledger Folio.	Bank.	Discount.	Cash.

The above example is from a colliery, and the columns headed "Railway Bank," "Yard," and "Agency" are for recording money received on account of the coal sold from the colliery direct, from land sales (yard), and through agency respectively. In the case of a metalliferous mine, the same form would do, but these columns would not be necessary.

The Cash Book proper is relieved from the details of very small items of expenditure by a "Petty Cash Book." Small amounts are from time to time credited to "Petty Cash Accounts" in the Cash Book, and the details of the spending of these sums are recorded in the **Petty Cash Book**. The petty cash expenditure can afterwards be analysed, if necessary, and posted into the ledger through the journal, or kept in a tabulated book.

Bills Receivable Account and Bills Payable Account.—Money owing may be paid by means of cash, by cheques, or by bills of exchange. In the case of cash, the amount is entered at once into the Cash Book; and similarly in the case of a cheque; for a cheque, being an order to pay the money on demand, is equivalent to cash. A bill, however, is a different matter; it is either a promise to pay the money at a future date, or an order on a third party to pay the money at some future date; so that when a bill is received, the amount cannot be posted in the Cash Book as cash received, but it is entered in a **Bills Receivable Book**. So, when a bill is given, it is entered in a **Bills Payable Book**, and if not specially ruled (see p. 93) the totals from these two books would be posted periodically to two corresponding accounts in the Ledger.

It does not follow that the party who receives a bill waits till the period when it falls due for payment. If the credit of the person who has drawn the bill is good, and also that of the person on whom it is drawn, then it is possible to get it paid at a bank *minus* a percentage for interest. This is called **discounting** a bill, the deduction made being the **discount**.

The following are two examples of bills :—

WHITEHAVEN, 2nd June, 1895.

£530 0 0

One month after date I promise to pay to Messrs. Hargreaves & Co. or their order the sum of Five hundred and thirty pounds for value received.

JOHN BROWN.

DERBY, 23rd May, 1895.

£375 0 0

Three months after date pay Messrs. Jones or their order the sum of Three hundred and seventy-five pounds for value received.

J. GREEN.

To Messrs. Black & White,
 Sheffield.

Bills of the former kind are often spoken of as **promissory notes**.

In the second example J. Green, called the **drawer**, draws a bill on Messrs. Black & White, the **drawees**, who are under some obligation to him, in favour of Messrs. Jones, the **payees**. This bill would be sent to Messrs.

HEAD OFFICE BOOKS.

Jones who would take it to Messrs. Black & White to see if they were prepared to make payment at the time specified. If they were prepared they would write across "accepted," specifying where payment would be made. They would then be known as the **acceptors**.

By writing his name on the back of a bill, that is **endorsing** it, the payee transfers his interest, and becomes responsible for the payment of the bill. If he also writes the name of another person on the back, he "specially" endorses it, and it is then payable to this person only; but if he only writes his own name, then the bill can pass from hand to hand.

Payment of a bill cannot be demanded till it is apparently three days overdue, these days being called **days of grace.**

The following is an example of a Foreign Bill payable abroad; it is usually made out in triplicate in case one of the copies should be lost in transmission. Should the first copy not reach its destination, the second, arriving by the following mail, would be paid on presentation in accordance with the wording. The third copy is retained till either the first or the second is duly acknowledged, when it is of no further use :—

LONDON, July 12, 1895.

Exchange for £360 15 0

One month after sight of this First of Exchange (second and third of same tenor and date unpaid) pay to William Brown or his order at the current rate of Exchange when due, Three hundred and sixty pounds fifteen shillings sterling for value received.

W. WILLIAMS.

To Messrs. Jackson & Co.,
Bombay.

The particular form in which a bill of exchange is drawn up varies with the circumstances of the case and with individual taste, considerable variation being admissible.

The following form of "Bills Receivable Book" will now be readily understood :—

Ledger Folio.	Number.	When received.	Of whom received.	By whom drawn.	On whom drawn.	To whom payable.	Where payable.	Date.	Term.	Due.	Amount.	How Disposed of.

The "Bills Payable Book" would be exactly similar in character, with the necessary slight alterations in the headings of columns.

Discount and Interest Account.—It was explained in the Chapter on "Stores" that 2½ per cent. was generally allowed when payment for goods was made within a month. This would be allowed *to* a company on stores and material bought, and might be allowed *by* a company on product sold. If accounts were much overdue, interest might be charged. Although these transactions could be recorded completely in cash account and personal accounts, yet, in order to have a separate record, and to find the total effect of discount and interest, received or given, a separate account is often kept, provision being made for recording the details in the Cash Book, while totals are posted to a Ledger account.

Product Account.—This account is credited with the value of all products sold. If several products are disposed of from the mine, then there may be several product accounts. They are headed with the name of the product thus, "Coal," "Bullion," "Ore," &c., as the case may be.

Working Accounts.—Sometimes, in order to exhibit the cost of getting mineral and preparing it for the market side by side with the money received from its sale, a "working" account is opened, which is debited with all working costs, and credited with the value of all mineral sold. The difference between the two sides of the account will then give the gross profit or loss. Again, a number of working accounts may be opened, to shew the cost of the various departments, or of various stages in extraction from the mine and preparation for the market. Thus, at De Beers Consolidated Mines there is a ledger account for each of the heads in their analysis of costs (see pp. 68 and 69).

Profit and Loss, or Revenue Account.—This account is posted periodically as a preliminary to the making of a balance sheet. It is debited with all current expenditure and loss on working; and credited with all current income and profit on working. Though somewhat similar in character to a working account, it differs by having reference not only to expenditure and receipt connected with working, but also to *all* expenditure and receipt which is not connected with capital. When there is a Working account, the profit and loss account is much shorter than otherwise, as it receives the balance from the Working account. Whereas, in the other case, it would receive in detail all the items which go into the Working account.

It will be readily seen that this account is of the very first interest to the Owner of a mine, or the Shareholders. Hence it is that The Companies Act, 1862, makes the following provisions in respect to it :— *

"Once at least in every year the Directors shall lay before the Company in General Meeting a Statement of the Income and Expenditure for the past year, made up to a date not more than three months before such Meeting."

"The Statement so made shall show, arranged under the most convenient heads, the amount of gross Income, distinguishing the several sources from which it has been derived, and the amount of gross Expenditure, distinguishing the expense of the establishment, salaries, and other like matters. Every item of expenditure, fairly chargeable against the year's income, shall be brought into account so that a just Balance of Profit and Loss may be laid before the Meeting; and, in cases where any item of expenditure which may in fairness be distributed over several years has been incurred in any one year, the whole amount of such item shall be stated, with the addition of the reasons why only a portion of such expenditure is charged against the income of the year."

The following is a simple form of Revenue Account used by a Colliery Company: sheets, with this and a form for a balance sheet printed on them, are kept in stock, and each half year they are filled in in writing, the number of shareholders not being very great:—

REVENUE ACCOUNT.

To Stock of Coal on hand, 18		By Gross Sales of Coal,	.	.
,, Mine Rents, .	. . .	,, Cottage Rents,	.	.
,, Salaries, .	. . .	,, Carting Account,	.	.
,, Wages, .	. . .	,, Manure,	.	.
,, Rates and Taxes, .	. .	,, Railway Rates,	.	.
,, Interest and Discounts, .	.	,, Waggon Account,	.	.
,, Directors' Fees, .	. .	,, Lamps,	.	.
,, Tradesmen's Bills, .	. .	,, Wick Account,	.	.
,, Incidental Expenses, .	.			
To Profit and Loss, .	.	,, Stock of Coal on hand, 18		

The next example † (see pp. 88 and 89) is taken from the Annual Report of

* First Schedule, Table A, pars. 79 and 80.
† For another example see p. 101 (Profit and Loss Account).

HEAD OFFICE BOOKS. 87

a Silver Mining Company, the chief office being in London and the mine abroad.

Instead of transferring the balances of the Revenue Account to the Balance Sheet, the whole account may be incorporated. This is not infrequently done in the early life of a Company when the property is being developed.

Having given details of such accounts as are generally found useful in keeping the permanent record of mines and mining transactions, we will now consider the books, other than those already described, which are necessary. A very useful help is a **Waste Book** (for example see p. 92), which is simply a memorandum of transactions as they occur, without reference to the manner in which they will be subsequently treated—a scribbling diary being a useful book for the purpose, if none other can be conveniently obtained. This must not be looked upon as one of the books absolutely necessary, but as a useful accessory.

A most essential book, on the other hand, is **The Journal**. This book could be employed to record every transaction. In modern practice, however, it only comes into use to record such transactions as cannot be put through subsidiary books, such as the Day Book or Purchase Book, &c. Such books may, in fact, be considered as forming part of the Journal.

A very usual form of journal is as follows, the first few transactions on p. 92 being entered for illustration:—

Date.			Ledger Folio.	Drs.			Crs.		
				£	s.	d.	£	s.	d.
1896.	Petty Cash.	Dr.		5	0	0			
Jan. 2,	To Cash.						5	0	0
Jan. 4,	Insurance.	Dr.		7	15	0			
	To Cash.						7	15	0
Jan. 5,	Stores.	Dr.		50	0	0			
	To R. Johnstone for 200 lbs. of Dynamite at 5s. per lb.						50	0	0
Jan. 9,	Stores.	Dr.		6	5	0			
	To S. Myers for 300 lbs. of Candles at 5d. per lb.						6	5	0

The transactions are recorded one after the other in order of date, and, by having two money columns to the right, one for debits, the other for credits, the two aspects of each transaction are recorded together. When a page is finished, the sum of the entries in the debit column should equal that of the entries in the credit column, and so the accuracy of the entries on each page can be tested before passing on to the next.

THE..........................

Dr.   REVENUE ACCOUNT from

		£ s. d.	£ s. d.
To Mines Expenditure—			
Salaries, Wages, Materials and Stores, Freight, Timber, and General Expenses,			£26,048 0 2
„ London Expenditure—			
Rent, Rates, and Taxes,		£333 6 8	
Salaries,		366 13 4	
Legal Expenses,		4 4 0	
Auditors' Fee,		52 10 0	
Cables, Telegrams, Postages, and Sundry Expenses,		72 18 10	
Printing and Stationery,		47 6 0	
Shareholders' Meeting,		40 12 9	
Travelling Expenses,		31 15 6	
Fees to Directors,		1,000 0 0	
Fee and Expenses—Director's visit to the Mines,		230 0 0	
			2,179 7 1
„ Income Tax,			269 18 4
„ Balance carried down,			6,794 3 4
			£35,291 8 11
To Mines Buildings, Plant, and Machinery—Amount written off,			£2,000 0 0
„ Reserve Account,			6,000 0 0
„ Balance carried to Balance Sheet,			589 2 0
			£8,589 2 0

The ordinary form of journal is sometimes modified by placing the Dr.'s column to the left of the accounts' column, thus :—*

DR.		Ledger Folio.	Date and Transactions.	Ledger Folio.	CR.	
Totals.	Items.				Items.	Totals.

This form has the advantage of separating the debits from the credits, so that the entries are less likely to be confused.

If there is a comparatively small number of accounts other than personal, or if there are a few accounts which receive more items than the others, as, for instance, the Cash Account and the Merchandise Account in ordinary business, the single debit column can be replaced by two, three, or more columns headed with the names of these accounts; and the credit column can be dealt with similarly. Baker describes this form under the title of "Synoptic," † which, he says, may be simply a preliminary to the ledger, or may replace it, in part or altogether. He also gives more elaborate examples with many columns.

In America journals containing four, six, or even eight columns are used to show the transactions; but, by this increase of columns, the book becomes unwieldy; hence the adoption of "**Purchase Book**" and "**Sales**" or "**Day Book**" (before mentioned), putting the right- and left-hand columns respectively into separate books, as is now so frequently done in this country.

* Oriol, *Contabilidad Minera*, 1894, Madrid, p. 12.
† Baker, *System of Accounts*, Columbus, Ohio, 1876, p. 68.

HEAD OFFICE BOOKS.

COMPANY, LIMITED.
1st January to 31st December, 1894. Cr.

By *Sales of Ore*—
  Realised to 31st December, ... £20,280 11 5
  Outstanding at 31st December—
    ....Smelting Company, . £11,301 15 3
    Other Smelters (since received), . 3,339 4 0
                                      ─────────── 14,640 19 3
                                                  ─────────── £34,921 10 8
,, *Transfer Fees and Sundry Receipts*, ... 29 0 0
,, *Interest on Loans*, ... 157 14 4
,, *Rent of Boarding Houses, at Mines*, ... 192 3 11

£35,291 8 11

By *Balance brought down*, ... £6,794 3 4
,, *Balance from Revenue Account, 1893*, . 1,794 18 8

£8,589 2 0

An example of each from an iron-ore mine, which, in addition to iron ore also sells loam sand, is as follows:—

PURCHASE JOURNAL.

				CREDITS.				DEBITS.						
Date.	No. of Invoice.	Name.	Description.	Amount.	Led. Folio.	Wages.	Railway Dues.	Damages.	Rent, Rates, &c.	Royalty.	Coals.	Stores.	Timber.
				£ s. d.		£ s. d.	£ s. d.	£ s. d.	£ s. d.	£ s. d.	£ s. d.	£ s. d.	£ s. d.
Jan. 9,		S. Myers,	Candles, 300 lbs. @ 5d.,	6 5 0							6 5 0		
Jan. 12,		A. Wilson,	Larch, 200 tons @ 35/,	350 0 0								350 0 0	
Jan. 12,		A. Walker,	Nails, 2 cwts. @ 12/6,	1 5 0								1 5 0	
Jan. 15,		G. Moss,	Coal, 50 tons @ 15/,	37 10 0							37 10 0		

SALES JOURNAL.

DEBITS.   CREDITS.

In the purchase journal, the names of the persons or firms from whom stores, &c., are bought—that is, the names of the Personal Accounts to be credited—are written in the column headed "Name," one after the other; the particulars of goods and amount due being entered in their respective columns, headed "Description" and "Amount," from the invoices. At the same time, each amount is entered in one of the columns under "debits," according to the particular account it must be debited to.

At the end of the month, a line is drawn right across the journal below all entries, and the vertical debit columns are added up; the horizontal sum of these totals should equal the total of the credits column headed "amount," and the necessary check is thus obtained. If the two general totals agree, then the totals of the debit columns are posted to their respective accounts in the ledger, the ledger folio being written just underneath each; the credit amounts are also posted, but in their case the ledger folios are written in the column provided at the side. A few explanatory entries are made in the Purchase Journal. One or two extra columns without headings may be provided, so that the name of any account only required at intervals can be written in.

An example of a Sales Journal for coal was given on p. 52, and the Day-book (p. 52) and Monthly Abstract (p. 53) described in the same connection are similar in character.

The Inventory.—This, as a rule, is a list of the property belonging to a Company. The value of the property is always represented in the ledger, but the inventory contains much fuller details than could be put into the ledger.

Balance Sheet.—We now pass on to consider the preparation of the Annual or Periodical Accounts, to be submitted to the proprietors.

The first step is, to take out what is technically called a "Trial Balance," which shews either the total posted to each account in the Ledger, or the Balance on open accounts only (see p. 101). If no error has been made, the debits and credits will be found, on adding up, to exhibit the same total.

The next step is to carefully consider the position of each account, and what items are necessary to adjust it. The Personal Accounts should simply require ruling off, as shewn on examples, pp. 99 and 100. The Balances, if any, are carried down, as shewn in *italics*. The Real and Nominal Accounts will, however, require more thought; but if the "Coal and Lead Ore Accounts" on p. 98 are referred to and studied, the method of treating them will be understood. The Manager having furnished the stock sheets shewing the stock of Coal, and also that of Lead Ore on hand, the amount is entered to the credit, and carried down to start the next period as a debit, thus obtaining the double entry. The difference then shewn is the amount transferable to the Working Account. For convenience of reference, these items are shewn in our example in *italics*.

The several closing entries are set out in the Journal, and the student must always remember that on no account can any prime entry be made in the Ledger *direct*; it should only be posted into the latter from a subsidiary book.

After the accounts have been adjusted, the "Working" and "Profit and Loss" Accounts will have come into existence by the posting of the several Journal entries, and the balances which then remain will form the basis of the Balance Sheet, which, in its simplest form, may be considered as a statement of Assets and Liabilities; explanation and details being afforded by the Profit and Loss Account. A form of Balance Sheet is attached to Table A in The Companies Act, 1862.

Although it would appear somewhat strange to see a balance sheet issued in Britain in any other form than the one given, yet it does not follow that this is

HEAD OFFICE BOOKS. 91

the best possible form in every case; and it may be drawn up very differently. The following is a good example from Colorado:—

..........................SMELTING AND MINING Co.
........................Colorado.
Balance Sheet, Taken........................18......

Accounts.	Trial Balance.		Inventory.	Representative.		Real.	
	Dr.	Cr.		Loss.	Gain.	Resources.	Liabilities.

The second and third columns are for the trial balance; then there is a column, headed "Inventory," for the value of the property—mine, plant, buildings, stocks, &c. The remaining four columns are for ledger balances, two for the nominal accounts and two for the real accounts. It is these ledger balances alone which are put into the balance sheet in this country.

Cost Book Mines never publish or even make a Balance Sheet. A financial statement similar in character to a Revenue Account is issued (see p. 86).

EXAMPLE.

The following Example will serve to illustrate the method of opening the books of a Company which has been formed to purchase a Mine and work it:—

GLEN LEAD MINING COMPANY, LIMITED.

CAPITAL, £50,000—
    In 50,000 shares of £1 each.

CONSIDERATION: £40,000.
    £10,000 in fully paid shares of the Company, and
    £30,000 cash payable in two instalments:—
        £10,000 on 1st December, 1895.
        £20,000 on 1st January, 1896.
Agreement signed on November 1st, 1895.

40,000 shares to be issued to the public, payment for which is to be made as follows:—
    5s. on application.
    7s. 6d. on allotment.
    7s. 6d. one month after allotment.

1895.	
Nov. 12th.	Received application for 24,000 shares.
,, 13th.	,, ,, ,, 16,000 shares.
,, 15th.	Allotted 10,000 fully paid shares to Vendors (or their nominees), and 40,000 to public, as per allotment book.
,, 18th.	Received £12,000 of the instalment due on allotment; being 7s. 6d. per share on 32,000 of the 40,000 allotted.
,, 19th.	,, £3,000, remainder of instalment due on allotment; being 7s. 6d. per share on 8000 shares.
Dec. 14th.	,, £9,000 of final instalment; being 7s. 6d. per share on 24,000 shares.
,, 15th.	,, £6,000, remainder of final instalment; being 7s. 6d. per share on 16,000 shares.

MINE ACCOUNTS.

During January the following transactions are presumed to have taken place:—

1896.

Date		Description	£	s.	D.
Jan.	2nd.	Paid to Clerk for petty cash,	5	0	0
,,	4th.	Paid Insurance Premium,	7	15	0
,,	5th.	Received from R. Johnstone 1,000 lbs. of dynamite at 1s. per lb.,	50	0	0
,,	9th.	Received from S. Myers 300 lbs. of candles at 5d. per lb.,	6	5	0
		Agreed to purchase plant and machinery from S. Jones & Co., for	4750	0	0
,,	9th.	Sold 40 tons of lead ore to the Roughton Smelting Co. at £7 10s. per ton,	300	0	0
,,	12th.	Bought of A. Wilson 200 tons of larch at 35s. per ton,	350	0	0
,,	12th.	Received from A. Walker 2 cwts. nails at 12s. 6d. per cwt.,	1	5	0
,,	12th.	Received 1 month's bill from the Roughton Smelting Co. in payment for lead ore,	300	0	0
,,	12th.	Discounted above bill; received	298	14	0
		Discount,	1	6	0
,,	14th.	Paid wages as per pay sheet (gross),	150	5	0
,,	14th.	Deductions—Cottage Rents,	4	0	0
,,	15th.	Received 50 tons coal from G. Moss at 15s. per ton,	37	10	0
,,	23rd.	Paid R. Johnstone's account, - £50 0 0			
		Less 2½ per cent. discount, - 1 5 0			
			48	15	0
,,	23rd.	Paid S. Myers' account, - - £6 5 0			
		Less 2½ per cent. discount, - 0 3 2			
			6	1	10
,,	23rd.	Gave A. Wilson a 3 months' bill for £350,	350	0	0
,,	23rd.	Paid A. Walker's account, - £1 5 0			
		Less 2½ per cent. discount, - 0 0 7			
			1	4	5
,,	23rd.	Paid G. Moss's account, - - £37 10 0			
		Less 2½ per cent. discount, - 0 18 9			
			36	11	3
,,	23rd.	Paid S. Jones & Co. for plant and machinery as agreed,	4,750	0	0
,,	24th.	Sold 25 tons of lead ore to the Roughton Smelting Co. at £7 15s. per ton,	193	15	0
,,	25th.	Received from John Stevenson—			
		40 gallons of engine oil at 2s. per gallon,	4	0	0
		40 gallons of lubricine at 1s. per gallon,	2	0	0
,,	25th.	Received from A. Walker—			
		1 dozen spades at 30s. per dozen,	1	10	0
		2 cwt. drill steel at 20s. per cwt.,	2	0	0
,,	25th.	Sold to Z. Levi old iron,	5	0	0
,,	27th.	Received a 1 month's bill from the Roughton Smelting Co. in payment for lead ore,	193	15	0
,,	28th.	Paid wages as per pay sheet (gross),	143	10	0
		Deductions for cottage rents,	4	0	0
,,	31st.	Paid Salaries—			
		Manager, - - - - £15 0 0			
		Clerk, - - - - - 6 0 0			
			21	0	0

The Stocks on 31st January we will assume to be—

	£
Stores estimated at	40
Timber, 160 tons at 35s.,	280
Coal, 20 tons at 15s.,	15
Lead Ore, 15 tons at £5,	75

Stores unused may fairly be valued at cost price; a good margin should always be allowed on the value of any product in stock. The value of stocks at the end of each period of work are recorded in a Stock-book.

CASH-BOOK.

Date.		Led. Fol.	Dis- count.	Cash		Date		Led. Fol.	Dis- count.		Cash.	
			£ s. d.	£	s. d.				£	s. d.	£	s. d.
1895. Nov. 12.	To Application A/c. (as per Allotment Book),			6,000	0 0	1895. Dec. 1.	By Purchase A/c., First instalment of the £30,000 to be paid in cash to the Vendor as per agreement dated Nov.1,1895				10,000	0 0
,, 13.	,, Application A/c. (as per do.),			4,000	0 0							
,, 18.	,, Allotment A/c. (as per do.),			12,000	0 0	1896. Jan. 1.	,, Purchase A/c., Final instalment of the £30,000 to be paid in cash to the Vendor as per agreement dated Nov.1,1895				20,000	0 0
,, 19.	,, Allotment A/c. (as per do.),			3,000	0 0							
Dec. 14.	,, Final Instalment A/c. (as per do.),			9,000	0 0							
,, 15.	,, Final Instalment A/c. (as per do.),			6,000	0 0	,, ,,	,, **Balance,**				10,000	0 0
				40,000	0 0						40,000	0 0
1896. Jan. 1.	To **Balance,**			10,000	0 0	1896. Jan. 1.	By Deposit A/c.,				5,000	0 0
,, 12.	,, Bills Receivable discounted,		1 6 0	298	14 0	,, 2.	,, Petty Cash,				5	0 0
,, 14.	,, Cottage Rents,			4	0 0	,, 4.	,, Insurance,				7	15 0
,, 28.	,, ,, ,,			4	0 0	,, 14.	,, Wages,				150	5 0
						,, 23.	,, R. Johnstone,		1	5 0	48	15 0
						,, ,,	,, S. Myers,		0	3 2	1	10
						,, ,,	,, A. Walker,		0	0 7	4	5
						,, ,,	,, G. Moss,		0	18 9	36	11 3
						,, ,,	,, S. Jones & Co.,				4,750	0 0
						,, 28.	,, Wages,				143	10 0
						,, 31.	,, Salaries— Manager,				15	0 0
						,, ,,	Clerk,				6	0 0
											10,170	2 6
							,, **Balance,**				136	11 6
			1 6 0	10,306	14 0				2	7 6	10,306	14 0

BILLS RECEIVABLE BOOK.

Number.	When Received.	Of whom Received.	By whom Drawn.	On whom Drawn.	To whom Payable.	Where Payable.	Date.	Term.	Due.	Led. Fo.	Amount.	Date.	Fo.	Amount.
											£ s. d.	1896.	By Jan. 12, Bank,	£ s. d.
	1896. Jan. 12,	Roughton Smelting Co.,	Them- selves,	Brown's Bank,	Our- selves,	Roughton	Jan. 11,	1 month,	Feb. 14,		300 0 0	Jan. 12,	By Dis.,	298 14 0
														1 6 0
	Jan. 27,	Roughton Smelting Co.,	Them- selves,	Brown's Bank,	Our- selves,	Roughton	Jan. 26,	1 month,	Mar. 1,		193 15 0			
											493 15 0			

BILLS PAYABLE BOOK.

Date.	Amount.	Number.	When Accepted.	By whom Drawn.	Place.	To whom Payable.	On whose Account.	Date.	Term.	Due.	Amount.	Led. Fo.	To whom
	£ s. d.							1896.			£ s. d.		
				Our- selves,	Glen,	A. Wilson,	Brown's Bank,	Jan. 23,	3 months,	Apl. 26,	350 0 0		
											350 0 0		

We will journalise the Capital transactions, sales, and closing entries in a two-column journal, and the purchases in a tabular journal as follows :—

JOURNAL.

Date.		Ledger Folio.	Drs.			Crs.		
			£	s.	D.	£	s.	D.
1895. Nov. 15.	Mines, Dr., ... To Purchase Account, . . Amount agreed to be paid for the Mines as per agreement dated 1st November, 1895, viz.: £30,000 cash in two instalments— On Dec. 1, 1895, £10,000. On Jan. 1, 1896, £20,000. £10,000 in fully paid shares. £40,000		40,000	0	0	40,000	0	0
Nov. 15.	Purchase Account, Dr., . . To Capital, ... For 10,000 fully paid shares allotted to the vendors (or their nominees), as above.		10,000	0	0	10,000	0	0
Nov. 15.	Application Account, Dr., . . To Capital, ... 5s. per share on application for the 40,000 shares to be issued to the public.		10,000	0	0	10,000	0	0
Dec. 15.	Allotment Account, Dr., . . To Capital, ... 7s. 6d. per share paid on allotment of 40,000 shares to the public.		15,000	0	0	15,000	0	0
Dec. 15.	Final Instalment Account, Dr., . To Capital, ... 7s. 6d. per share on 40,000 shares paid one month after allotment.		15,000	0	0	15,000	0	0
1896. Jan. 9.	Plant and Machinery, Dr., . . To S. Jones & Co., . . For agreed price at which same taken over by Company.		4,750	0	0	4,750	0	0
Jan. 9.	Roughton Smelting Co., Dr., . To Lead Ore, ... For 40 tons of lead ore at £7, 10s. per ton.		300	0	0	300	0	0
Jan. 24.	Roughton Smelting Co., Dr., . To Lead Ore, ... For 25 tons lead ore at £7, 15s. per ton.		193	15	0	193	15	0

HEAD OFFICE BOOKS.

Date.		Ledger Folio.	Drs.			Crs.		
			£	s.	D.	£	s.	D.
Jan. 25.	Z. Levi, Dr., To Stores, For old iron.		5	0	0	5	0	0
Jan. 31.	Discount Account, Dr., To Profit and Loss Account, For balance transferred.		1	1	6	1	1	6
	Profit and Loss Account, Dr., To Petty Cash Account, For balance transferred.		5	0	0	5	0	0
	Profit and Loss Account, Dr., To Insurance Account, For balance transferred.		7	15	0	7	15	0
	Working Account, Dr., To Stores Account, For balance transferred.		22	0	0	22	0	0
	Working Account, Dr., To Timber, For balance transferred.		70	0	0	70	0	0
	Working Account, Dr., To Coal, For balance transferred.		22	10	0	22	10	0
	Lead Ore Account, Dr., To Working Account, For balance transferred.		568	15	0	568	15	0
	Cottage Rents Account, Dr., To Profit and Loss Account, For balance transferred.		8	0	0	8	0	0
	Working Account, Dr., To Wages Account, For balance transferred.		293	15	0	293	15	0
	Working Account, Dr., To Salaries Account, For balance transferred.		21	0	0	21	0	0
	Working Account, Dr., To Profit and Loss Account, For balance transferred.		139	10	0	139	10	0

BOUGHT JOURNAL.

		CREDITS.				DEBITS.		
Date.	Invoice No.	Name.	Description.	Amount.	Led. Fol.	Coal.	Stores.	Timber.
				£ s. d.	£ s. d.	£ s. d.	£ s. d.	£ s. d.
1896. Jan. 5.		R. Johnstone,	Dynamite,	50 0 0			50 0 0	
,, 9.		S. Myers,	Candles,	0 5 0			0 5 0	
,, 12.		A. Wilson,	Larch,	350 0 0				350 0 0
,, 12.		A. Walker,	Nails,	1 5 0			1 5 0	
,, 15		G. Moss,	Coal,	37 10 0		37 10 0		
,, 25.		J. Stevenson,	Oil,	6 0 0			6 0 0	
,, 25.		A. Walker,	Spades and Steel,	3 10 0			3 10 0	
				454 10 0		37 10 0	67 0 0	350 0 0

LEDGER.

Dr.   CAPITAL.   Cr.

£ s. D.	1895.		£	S. D.
	Nov. 15,	By Purchase A/c,	10,000	0 0
		,, Application A/c,	10,000	0 0
		,, Allotment A/c,	15,000	0 0
	Dec. 15,	,, Final Instalment A/c,	15,000	0 0
			50,000	0 0

Dr.   PURCHASE.   Cr.

1895.			£ s. D.	1895.			£	S. D.
Nov. 15,	To Capital,		10,000 0 0	Nov. 15,	By Mines,		40,000	0 0
Dec. 1,	,, Cash,		10,000 0 0					
1896. Jan. 1,	,, Cash,		20,000 0 0					
			40,000 0 0				40,000	0 0

Dr.   MINES.   Cr.

1895.			£	S. D.
Nov. 15,	To Purchase,	-	40,000	0 0

Dr.   APPLICATION.   Cr.

1895.		£	S. D.	1895.		£	S. D.
Nov. 15,	To Capital,	10,000	0 0	Nov. 12,	By Cash,	6,000	0 0
				Nov. 13,	,, Cash,	4,000	0 0
		10,000	0 0			10,000	0 0

Allotment.

Dr.								Cr.		
1895.			£	s.	D.	1895.		£	s.	D.
Nov. 19,	To Capital,	-	15,000	0	0	Nov. 18,	By Cash, - -	12,000	0	0
						,, 19,	,, Cash, - -	3,000	0	0
			15,000	0	0			15,000	0	0

Final Instalment.

Dr.								Cr.		
1895.			£	s.	D.	1895.		£	s.	D.
Dec. 15,	To Capital,	-	15,000	0	0	Dec. 14,	By Cash, - -	9,000	0	0
						,, 15,	,, Cash, - -	6,000	0	0
			15,000	0	0			15,000	0	0

Plant and Machinery.

Dr.						Cr.
1896.			£	s.	D.	
Jan. 9,	To S. Jones & Co.,		4,750	0	0	

S. Jones & Co.

Dr.								Cr.		
1896.			£	s.	D.	1896.		£	s.	D.
Jan. 23,	To Cash, - -		4,750	0	0	Jan. 9,	By Plant and Machinery,	4,750	0	0

Discount.

Dr.								Cr.		
1896.			£	s.	D.	1896.		£	s.	D.
Jan. 31,	To Sundries (as per Cash Book),		1	6	0	Jan. 31,	By Sundries (as per Cash Book),	2	7	6
	,, Profit and Loss A/c., . .		1	1	6					
			2	7	6			2	7	6

Petty Cash.

Dr.								Cr.		
1896.			£	s.	D.	1896.		£	s.	D.
Jan. 2,	To Cash, . .		5	0	0	Jan. 31,	By Profit and Loss A/c., . .	5	0	0
			5	0	0			5	0	0

Insurance.

Dr.								Cr.		
1896.			£	s.	D.	1896.		£	s.	D.
Jan. 4,	To Cash, . .		7	15	0	Jan. 31,	By Profit and Loss A/c., . .	7	15	0
			7	15	0			7	15	0

Dr. STORES. Cr.

1896.		£	s.	D.	1896.		£	s.	D.
Jan. 5,	To R. Johnstone,	50	0	0	Jan. 25,	By Z. Levi,	5	0	0
,, 9,	,, S. Myers,	6	5	0	Jan. 31,	,, Working A/c.,	22	0	0
,, 12,	,, A. Walker,	1	5	0	,, 31,	,, Stock carried			
,, 25,	,, J. Stevenson,	6	0	0		down, . .	40	0	0
	,, A. Walker,	3	10	0					
		67	0	0			67	0	0
Feb. 1,	,, Stock brought down. .	40	0	0					

Dr. TIMBER. Cr.

1896.		£	s.	D.	1896.		£	s.	D.
Jan. 12,	To A. Wilson,	350	0	0	Jan. 31,	By Working A/c.,	70	0	0
					,, 31,	,, Stock carried down, . .	280	0	0
		350	0	0			350	0	0
Feb. 1,	,, Stock brought down, . .	280	0	0					

Dr. COAL. Cr.

1896.		£	s.	D.	1896.		£	s.	D.
Jan. 15,	To G. Moss,	37	10	0	Jan. 31,	By Working A/c.,	22	10	0
					,, 31,	,, Stock carried down, . .	15	0	0
		37	10	0			37	10	0
Feb. 1,	,, Stock brought down, . .	15	0	0					

Dr. LEAD ORE. Cr.

1896.		£	s.	D.	1896.		£	s.	D.
Jan. 31,	To Working A/c.,	568	15	0	Jan. 9,	By Roughton Smelting Co.,	300	0	0
					,, 24,	,, Roughton Smelting Co.,	193	15	0
					Jan. 31,	,, Stock carried down, . .	75	0	0
		568	15	0			568	15	0
Feb. 1,	,, Stock brought down, . .	75	0	0					

Dr. COTTAGE RENTS. Cr.

1896.		£	s.	D.	1896.		£	s.	D.
Jan. 31,	To Profit and Loss A/c., . .	8	0	0	Jan. 14,	By Cash, .	4	0	0
					,, 28,	,, Cash, .	4	0	0
		8	0	0			8	0	0

Dr.					WAGES.			Cr.		
1896.		£	s.	D.	1896.		£	s.	D.
Jan. 14,	To Cash,	150	5	0	Jan. 31,	By Working A/c.,	293	15	0
,, 28,	,, Cash,	143	10	0					
		293	15	0			293	15	0

Dr.					SALARIES.			Cr.		
1896.		£	s.	D.	1896.		£	s.	D.
Jan. 31,	To Cash,	21	0	0	Jan. 31,	By Working A/c.,	21	0	0
		21	0	0			21	0	0

Dr.					DEPOSIT ACCOUNT.			Cr.		
1896.		£	s.	D.			£	s.	D.
Jan. 1,	To Cash,	5,000	0	0					

Dr.					R. JOHNSTONE.			Cr.		
1896.		£	s.	D.	1896.		£	s.	D.
Jan. 23,	To Cash,	48	15	0	Jan. 5,	By Stores,	50	0	0
,, 23,	To Discount,	1	5	0					
		50	0	0			50	0	0

Dr.					S. MYERS.			Cr.		
1896.		£	s.	D.	1896.		£	s.	D.
Jan. 23,	To Cash,	6	1	10	Jan. 9,	By Stores,	6	5	0
	,, Discount,	0	3	2					
		6	5	0			6	5	0

Dr.					ROUGHTON SMELTING CO.			Cr.		
1896.		£	s.	D.	1896.		£	s.	D.
Jan. 9,	To Lead Ore,	300	0	0	Jan. 12,	By Bills Receivable,	300	0	0
,, 24,	,, Lead Ore,	193	15	0	,, 27,	,, Bills Receivable,	193	15	0
		493	15	0			493	15	0

A. WILSON.

Dr.			£	s.	D.				£	s.	D.	Cr.
1896. Jan. 23,	To Bills Payable,		350	0	0	1896. Jan. 12,	By Timber,	-	350	0	0	
			350	0	0				350	0	0	

A. WALKER.

Dr.			£	s.	D.				£	s.	D.	Cr.
1896. Jan. 23,	To Cash,	-	1	4	5	1896. Jan. 12,	By Stores,	-	1	5	0	
	,, Discount,	-	0	0	7	,, 25,	,, Stores,	-	3	10	0	
Jan. 31,	,, Balance carried down,	-	3	10	0							
			4	15	0				4	15	0	
						Feb. 1,	,, Balance brought down,		3	10	0	

G. MOSS.

Dr.			£	s.	D.				£	s.	D.	Cr.
1896. Jan. 23,	To Cash,	-	36	11	3	1896. Jan. 15,	By Coal,	-	37	10	0	
	,, Discount,	-	0	18	9							
			37	10	0				37	10	0	

JOHN STEVENSON.

Dr.			£	s.	D.				£	s.	D.	Cr.
1896. Jan. 31,	To Balance carried down,	-	6	0	0	1896. Jan. 25,	By Stores,	-	6	0	0	
			6	0	0				6	0	0	
							,, Balance brought down,		6	0	0	

Z. LEVI.

Dr.			£	s.	D.				£	s.	D.	Cr.
1896. Jan. 25,	To Stores,	-	5	0	0	1896. Jan. 31,	By Balance carried down,	-	5	0	0	
			5	0	0				5	0	0	
Feb. 1,	,, Balance brought down,		5	0	0							

WORKING ACCOUNT.

Dr.			£	s.	D.				£	s.	D.	Cr.
1896. Jan. 31,	To Stores A/c.,		22	0	0	1896. Jan. 31,	By Lead Ore A/c.,		568	15	0	
	,, Timber ,,		70	0	0							
	,, Coal ,,		22	10	0							
	,, Wages ,,		293	15	0							
	,, Salaries ,,		21	0	0							
	,, Profit and Loss A/c., . .		139	10	0							
			568	15	0				568	15	0	

HEAD OFFICE BOOKS.

Dr. PROFIT AND LOSS ACCOUNT. Cr.

1896.		£	s.	D.	1896.		£	s.	D.
Jan. 31,	To Petty Cash A/c.,	5	0	0	Jan. 31,	By Discount A/c.,	1	1	6
	,, Insurance ,,	7	15	0		,, Cottage Rents ,,	8	0	0
	,, Balance carried down,	135	16	6		,, Working ,,	139	10	0
		148	11	6			148	11	6
					Feb. 1,	,, Balance brought down,	135	16	6

TRIAL BALANCE.

Ledger Folio.	Account.	Dr.			Cr.		
		£	s.	D.	£	s.	D.
	Capital,				50,000	0	0
	Mine,	40,000	0	0			
	Machinery and Plant,	4,750	0	0			
	Deposit Account,	5,000	0	0			
	Bank Account,	136	11	6			
	Discount,				1	1	6
	Bills Receivable,	193	15	0			
	Bills Payable,				350	0	0
	Petty Cash,	5	0	0			
	Insurance,	7	15	0			
	Stores,	62	0	0			
	Timber,	350	0	0			
	Coal,	37	10	0			
	Lead Ore,				493	15	0
	Cottage Rents,				8	0	0
	Wages,	293	15	0			
	Salaries,	21	0	0			
	A. Walker,				3	10	0
	J. Stevenson,				6	0	0
	Z. Levi,	5	0	0			
		50,862	6	6	50,862	6	6

GLEN LEAD MINING COMPANY,

BALANCE SHEET FOR MONTH ENDING JANUARY 31ST, 1895.

LIABILITIES.		£	s.	D.	ASSETS.		£	s.	D.
Capital—					Mine, for cost of same as a going concern,		40,000	0	0
Nominal Capital: 50,000 shares of £1 each.					Machinery,		4,750	0	0
Subscribed Capital: 50,000 shares of £1 each paid up,		50,000	0	0	Stocks— £ s. d. Stores, 40 0 0 Timber, 280 0 0				
Debts—					Coal, 15 0 0				
Bills Payable,		350	0	0	Ore, 75 0 0		410	0	0
Sundry Creditors— £ s. d. A. Walker, 3 10 0 J. Stevenson, 6 0 0		9	10	0	Deposit Account, Debts— Debtor: Z. Levi, Bills Receivable,		5,000 5 193	0 0 15	0 0 0
Profit and Loss Account,		135	16	6	Cash at Bank,		136	11	6
		£50,495	6	6			£50,495	6	6

BIBLIOGRAPHY.

Book-keeping.

Bickerstaff; Book-keeping Terms. London, 1890. pp. 47.
Carter; Practical Book-keeping, 6th Ed. Edinburgh, 1890. pp. 263.
Cummins; Book-keeping. Dublin, 1887.
Dicksee; Auditing, 2nd Ed. London, 1895. pp. 579.
Gay; Business Book-keeping. Boston, 1893.
Goodwin; Improved Book-keeping, 16th Ed. New York City, 1893. pp. 293.
Nixon; Longman's Advanced Book-keeping. London, 1894. pp. 366.
Norton; Textile Manufacturers' Book-keeping, 3rd Ed. London, 1894.
Pixley; Auditors, 6th Ed. London, 1891. pp. 245.
Pixley and **Wilson**; Book-keeping. London, 1892. pp. 112.
Thornton; A Manual of Book-keeping. London, 1895. pp. 527.
Van de Linde, Gérard; Book-keeping. London, 1891. pp. 150.
Whatley; The Accountants' and Book-keepers' Vade-Mecum. London, 1893. pp. 159.

Bills of Exchange.

Byles; Treatise on the Law of Bills of Exchange, 15th Ed. London, 1891. pp. 584.
Chalmers; Bills of Exchange, 4th Ed. London, 1891. pp. 431.
Chitty and **Russell**; A Practical Treatise on Bills of Exchange, 11th Ed. London, 1878.
Loyd; Four Lectures on Bills of Exchange. London, 1895. pp. 174.
Smith, J. W.; Law of Bills, Cheques, Notes, and I.O.U.'s, 58th thousand. London, 1894. pp. 193. A small handbook.

CHAPTER XI.—REDEMPTION OF CAPITAL.

WHEN work commences at a mine, there must necessarily be a period during which the expenditure is great and the income almost *nil;* this is the time during which the capital is spent and the capital expenditure accounts are growing. When the profitable stage is reached, it would not be considered satisfactory if the profit were such that the investor simply got bare interest on his money. He would naturally expect to be recouped for the loss of interest during the unproductive stage of the undertaking; further, the machinery put up is constantly depreciating in value, and if the mine lasts long enough may have to be replaced, for which, and for development work underground and at the surface, the investor does not expect to be asked for fresh capital; consequently there ought to be a surplus sufficient to meet current development expenses and to build up a reserve fund. This is not all; for a mine, even a rich mine, is not a permanent source of wealth; sooner or later it will be impossible to work it without loss, so that during the profitable period of its life, not only must interest be paid on the capital, but the capital itself must be paid back, if the mine is to be considered successful.

Generally speaking, the middle part of the life of a mine is the most profitable; towards its latter years the underground roads to be maintained get longer, or the mine gets deeper, and working expenses increase.

Redemption of Capital and Allowance for Depreciation may either be looked upon as identical, or a distinction may be made. In the first case, the amount of the capital is considered to be the value of the mine, buildings, plant, &c.,

taken as a whole; as the mineral is removed, although development may show riches which lead to a temporary appreciation, yet the inevitable ultimate result is a lessening in value, so that the laying aside of monies annually to counterbalance this, may be spoken of as redeeming capital or providing for depreciation. In the other case "depreciation" may be taken to refer to the value of the buildings, machinery, and plant which does not entirely depend on the life of the mine, while "redemption" refers to the capital otherwise invested or to the capital as a whole. We will make the distinction, and will consider in turn Redemption of Capital, Depreciation, and the Reserve Fund.

Redemption of Capital.—The first point to consider under this head is the life of a mine. Sometimes this can be determined within reasonable limits, at other times it is an entirely speculative quantity. In the case of a coal mine, the number and thickness of the coal seams being known from borings and, perhaps, from neighbouring mines, and the probable amount of faulting being known more or less from a knowledge of the neighbourhood, the quantity of workable coal can be estimated; then, by a careful balancing between minimum capital outlay and technical difficulties, on the one hand, and minimum working expenses, which means a large output, on the other hand, the quantity it is desirable to extract per week can be determined; and by dividing the total amount of workable coal by the output, the life of the colliery may be estimated, supposing the company is not hampered with a comparatively short lease and a hard landlord; if this is the case it may be best to consider that the lease determines the life of the colliery as far as concerns the company In a similar manner the life of many of the gold mines working beds of conglomerate on the Rand, of the mines working the thin bed of copper-bearing shale at Mansfeld, of the nitrate of soda workings in Chili can be estimated with a fair degree of approximation. In short, generally speaking, where the mineral deposit is in the form of a bed, the yield is more uniform than in other cases, and the production of a particular area of that bed can be approximately foretold.

Mass deposits are often capable of being satisfactorily dealt with in this particular, as they sometimes contain immense quantities of mineral, and although their exact boundaries cannot at once be traced, yet oftentimes it does not take long to find out sufficient about their dimensions to justify considerable outlay, and by pushing on exploration quickly by means of boreholes or shafts and drifts, their contents may be estimated and the life of a mine, at a certain rate of working, calculated. As examples, may be mentioned the hæmatite deposits of Furness and Cumberland, the cupreous pyrites at Rio Tinto, and the deposits of diamond-bearing rock at Kimberley.

Veins are generally variable and uncertain in their yield, and though they have been the source of immense riches in many cases, and will continue to be so vein-working is often a very speculative undertaking. The vein itself may be very irregular in size, sometimes nipping up till the two walls meet, and again opening out to a width of many feet. The ores are also often distributed through a vein in a very irregular manner, one portion of the vein being absolutely worthless, while a neighbouring portion may be very rich; so that, in an extreme case, a single day's work in a drift of hitherto valueless veinstone may reveal sufficient riches to pay back a good portion of the capital of a mining company in a few months.

Thus it will be seen that, in considering the life of a Mining Company, great care must be taken to carefully distinguish the character of the deposit. In some cases a good approximation is possible, and that even in the case of veins; in other cases, any attempt at estimation would be either a result of ignorance or a wilful attempt to mislead.

MINE ACCOUNTS.

Supposing the profits sufficiently large to redeem Capital, its repayment may be arranged in the following three ways:—

(1) **Part of the Capital may be issued as debentures**, a certain number of which fall due for payment each year; so that year by year a certain part of the Capital is paid off, and as the mine gets older the Capital on which interest has to be paid gets less. This method is especially applicable where it is necessary or advisable to enlarge the Capital subsequent to the formation of a Company, as, for instance, where development shows that it will be more profitable to work a mine on a larger scale than was at first intended. Sometimes debentures are all redeemable at the same time, in which case the necessary amount must be accumulated, as in the next method.

(2) **A certain sum may be put by every year** and invested, so that at the end of a number of years, equal to the estimated life of the mine, there will have accumulated an amount equal to the Capital, then, if the mine has to be abandoned, the shareholders may have their Capital returned, and the concern be wound up. Such an accumulating reserve is known as a **sinking fund**. It may be arranged for in various ways:—(A) An equal sum may be put by each year of the profitable life of the mine; (B) A varying annual sum may be put by, depending upon some formula adopted; (C) A varying sum may be put by each year, depending upon the proportion of the amount of mineral raised during the year to the whole of the mineral contained in the mine.

(A) **Equal Annual Sums.**—The problem is what amount must be put by each year and invested, so that in a certain number of years the accumulated sums shall equal the Capital.

Let x be equal yearly instalments necessary to redeem one pound in n years; and let R be the "amount" of one pound in one year, that is one pound *plus* interest for one year on it.

Then x put by at the end of the first year would in n years become $x R^{n-1}$; put by at the end of the second year it would accumulate to $x R^{n-2}$; so that we have at the end of the period one pound $= x R^{n-1} + x R^{n-2} + x R^{n-3} \ldots x R + x$; therefore—

$$1 = x (R^{n-1} + R^{n-2} \ldots R + 1)$$
$$= x \left(\frac{R^n - 1}{R - 1} \right)$$
$$x = \frac{R - 1}{R^n - 1}$$

If the mine was not profitable, say for three years, after its commencement, then n would equal the life of the mine less three years, and the capital to be redeemed would be the original capital with interest for three years added—that is CR_1^3—unless the profits were such that this accumulated interest could be paid off. R_1 would be at a higher rate than R, for better interest would be expected for the money invested in the mine than that at which the sinking fund could be safely invested.

The curves * on p. 105 show the relation between the number of years and the sum to be put by each year, for every pound of capital, when the redemption fund is invested at $1\frac{1}{2}$ or $2\frac{1}{2}$ per cent.

Thus suppose the redemption fund goes on accumulating for 25 years. Follow the horizontal line for 25 years till it intersects the curves, and it will be seen that if the fund is invested at $1\frac{1}{2}$ per cent. £·033 (nearly 8d. per pound) must be put by each year; whereas if it is invested at $2\frac{1}{2}$ per cent. it will only be necessary to put by £·0293 (about 7d.)

* Plotted from Table V. of Hoskold's *Engineer's Valuing Assistant*, London, 1877.

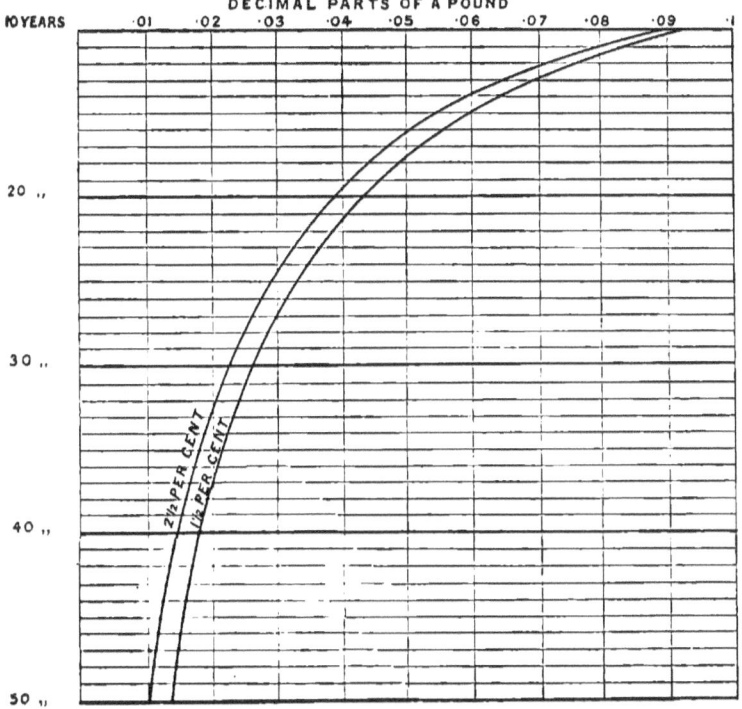

(B) **Annual sum varying according to a Formula.**—Mr. J. B. Smith * suggests that as the profits are generally better in the earlier and middle parts of the active exploitation of a mine, larger sums towards redemption of capital should be contributed during these periods than in the closing years of a mine's existence. He gives the following formula:—If a is the last sum put by, then $2a$ shall be the last but one, $3a$ the last but two; thus the series of instalments will be—

$$a, 2a, 3a, 4a, \ldots na.$$

Suppose these sums invested at compound interest, using the same letters as before, we have—

$$\text{Capital} = C = aR + 2a R^2 + 3a R^3 \ldots naR^n$$

$$= \frac{aR^{n+1}[n(R-1)-1] + aR}{(R-1)^2}$$

And

$$a = \frac{C(R-1)^2}{R^{n+1}[n(R-1)-1] + R}$$

As an example, suppose $C = £100,000$; lease, 55 years, $n = 55 - 5 = 50$; interest 2 per cent.; then

Last payment = £39, 4s. 3d.
First payment = £1,960, 12s. 6d.

---

* J. Bagnold Smith "On Colliery Depreciation." *Trans. Federated Institute of Mining Engineers*, vol. ii., p. 211.

(C) **Annual Sum Depending on Output of Mineral.**—Taking the case of a colliery, depreciation may be calculated from the amount of mineral worked away, either on tonnage or acreage, the amount of mineral originally in the mine having been calculated beforehand. Here is an example*—Capital, £70,000; term, 50 years; 1,000 acres of coal 6 feet thick; taking an acre 1 inch thick to yield 100 tons, the colliery ought to yield 7,200,000 tons of coal. Suppose removal value of plant when colliery is finished to be £5,000, then there is £65,000 to be recouped, which is 2·16d. per ton.

In all cases a better idea of the life of a mine, or amount of mineral to be won, can be obtained as work progresses, so that it will be necessary to re-calculate and adjust the sums to be put by each year, at intervals.

Comparing the above three methods, although advantages can be urged in favour of each, yet the general consensus of opinion † seems to be in favour of the first.

Although there is much to be said in favour of some method of accumulating a sinking fund such fund rarely exists in connection with mining companies. The money must necessarily be invested safely, and so the interest it bears is small, whereas the shareholders could invest it for themselves to better advantage if it were paid to them year by year, as they would generally be prepared to take greater risk than directors dare reasonably assume; and otherwise, it is but natural they should prefer having the money in hand to waiting till the end of a more or less lengthy term for it; thus we are led to the third method of arranging the redemption of capital.

(3) **Enlarged dividends, or dividends and bonuses**, may be paid, so that the shareholder receives a fair interest on his investment, and an additional sum each year which counts towards repayment of principal.

The problem may be put in three ways :—(1) Supposing a mining company is paying a certain sum annually, assuming a fair rate of interest on the investment, in **how many years** will the capital be repaid? (2) assuming a certain number of years as the profitable life of the mine, and a certain rate of interest, **what sum must be paid each year** in order to repay the capital in the number of years assumed? (3) assuming the number of years in the profitable life of the mine, and the sum paid each year, **what interest is being yielded** on capital invested? Thus it will be seen there are three variables, viz.:—The profitable life of the mine (n); the amount paid each year as dividend (x); and interest on capital (amount of one pound in one year, R). The relation between these three variables may be conveniently shown by means of curves.

The sum received each year as dividend may be looked upon as an annuity; and the capital invested, being the amount paid for the dividend, as the present value (P) of the annuity.

According to the ordinary rules,‡ we have—

$$P = \frac{R^n - 1}{R^n (R - 1)} x$$

and if we deal with £1 of capital

$$x^1 = \frac{R^n (R - 1)}{R^n - 1} \quad . \quad . \quad . \quad . \quad . \quad (1)$$

x^1 being the amount of dividend received for each £1 of capital.

* Evans, "Lecture on Colliery Accounts," *The Accountant*, vol. xii., 1886, p. 54. See also Attlee, "Lecture on Colliery Accounts," *The Accountant*, vol. xi., 1885, pp. 576-9; and Smith, *Op. cit.*

† See discussion on Mr. Smith's paper in *Trans. Fed. Inst. of Mining Engineers*, vol. iii., p. 119; also H. D. Hoskold, "Notes upon Redemption of Capital Invested in Collieries," *Trans. Fed. Inst. of Mining Engineers*, vol. iii., p. 735.

‡ See Todhunter's *Algebra*. London, 1887, p. 364.

REDEMPTION OF CAPITAL.

This method of solving the problem assumes that the amount of the annuity beyond the interest on capital, is invested each year at the same rate of interest as the capital yields. This is evidently unfair, for while 8 or 10 or even a greater percentage might not be considered too much for capital investment in mining, such capital could not safely be recouped at a greater interest than perhaps $2\frac{1}{2}$ or 2 per cent.

Let * r be the interest on one pound obtained from capital invested, then $R = 1 + r$; also let r^1 be the interest obtained on sums annually invested to recoup capital, and $r^1 + 1 = R_1$; the other symbols have the same significance as before. We may find the relation between x^1, n, r and r^1, thus:—

The annual interest on each pound of capital is r, so that the sum to be annually invested is $(x^1 - r)$. If A denote the amount of an annuity of £1·· accumulating at r^1 per cent., then—

$$(x^1 - r) A = 1$$

$$x^1 = \frac{1}{A} + r \qquad . \quad (2)$$

Now A is evidently given by the same formula as that for the sinking fund (p. 104), and remembering that $R_1 - 1 = r^1$ we have—

$$x^1 = \frac{r^1}{R_1^n - 1} + r \qquad (3)$$

In the extreme case where Capital accumulating is supposed to yield no interest, A would simply equal n; and from (2) we have—

$$x^1 = \frac{1}{n} + r$$

The following three sets of curves shew the relation between the three variables—years, dividends, and percentages paid on Capital—under the three assumptions above considered:—

WHEN CAPITAL IS RECOUPED AT THE SAME RATE OF INTEREST AS THAT PAID ON THE SHARES.

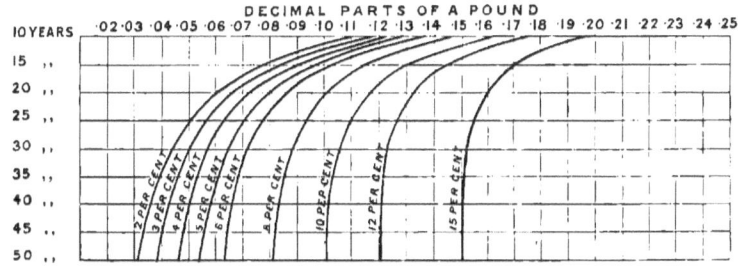

* The student will find this problem fully discussed by Hoskold, *Op. cit.*, pp. 31, 43 to 55; and also in the *Institute of Actuaries' Text-book*, by William Sutton, London, 1882, p. 31, *et seq.*

WHEN CAPITAL IS RECOUPED AT 2½ PER CENT. INTEREST.

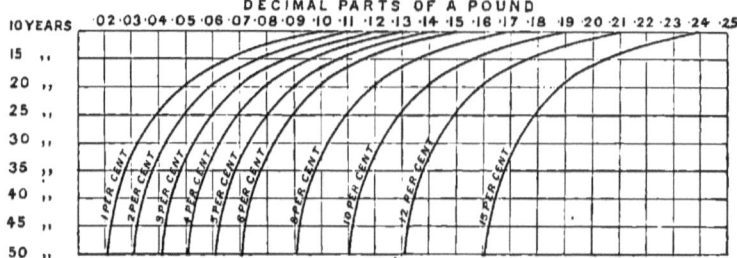

WHEN CAPITAL IS RECOUPED AT NO INTEREST.

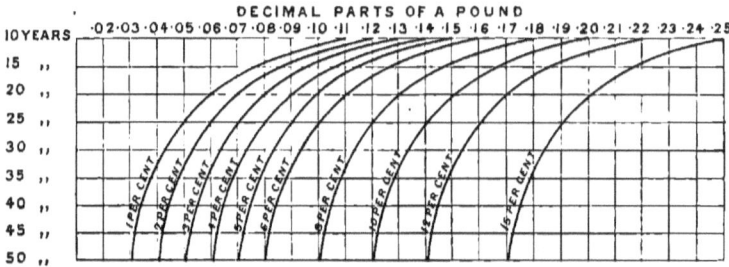

As an example of the use of these diagrams, suppose a dividend of 2s. per pound of capital is paid—an apparent 10 per cent.—and that the life of the mine is taken to be twenty years. Take the horizontal line for twenty years in each diagram, and the vertical line corresponding to 2s., that is ·1 of a pound. It will be seen that the intersection in the first diagram is near the 8 per cent. curve, so that under the conditions of the first diagram the dividend is barely 8 per cent. Under the conditions of the second diagram it is a little over 6 per cent., and of the third about 5 per cent. Thus the apparent 10 per cent. dividend is in truth, when the redemption of Capital is considered, only 8, or 6, or 5 per cent., according to the conditions under which it is considered that repaid Capital accumulates.

Again, suppose a company is paying annually 2s. per pound of Capital, and that 8 per cent. is considered a fair interest on money invested. In how many years will the Capital be repaid? Take the 8 per cent. curve in each diagram, and find its intersection with the ·1 vertical line. The position of this point in relation to the horizontal lines gives the number of years. Thus the first diagram gives it a trifle over twenty years; the second about thirty-two years; and the third fifty years.

Finally, suppose that the life of the mine is assumed to be thirty years, and that it is wished to pay 8 per cent. on Capital invested in addition to repaying the Capital. How much per pound must be paid each year? Find the intersection of the horizontal line for thirty years with the 8 per cent. curve, then the position of this point in relation to the vertical lines gives the amount. The first diagram gives ·0885 (1s. 9d.); the second ·1025 (2s. 0½d.); and the third ·114 (about 2s. 3d.).

When no dividend is paid for the first part of the life of a mine, the case may be looked upon as similar to that of a deferred annuity. Mr. Hoskold works out the problem,* and also gives present values of such annuities. The amounts required to plot curves, similar to those given above, for this case are the reciprocals of these present values.

For simplicity it has been supposed that interest has been paid, and investment of repaid Capital made, yearly. If the periods were shorter the results would be slightly different.

The trouble of this method of repaying Capital is that people do not, in general, sufficiently grasp the fact that a mine is a wasting, often a rapidly wasting, asset; when a dividend is paid it is spoken of as so much per cent. and looked upon as *interest* on the Capital; whereas, when provision has not otherwise been made for the redemption of Capital, a certain portion must first be laid aside before the shareholder can ascertain how much interest he has received. Few, except those who have paid special attention to the matter, properly apprehend the great difference between a dividend which is purely interest on Capital invested, as in many business concerns, and a dividend which is in part repayment of Capital; the calculations are somewhat intricate and lengthy, and the person interested either does not trouble about the matter at all, or makes a rough guess, which in all probability is far from the truth. Perhaps the graphic method illustrated above is the best for arriving at an approximately accurate result in the shortest time, with the least trouble, and with the least likelihood of error. Unfortunately, directors foster false impressions on this matter, rather than otherwise; the future of mines, perhaps temporarily successful, is rarely studied with the attention its importance deserves, and even such definite information as directors have, they do not put plainly before shareholders, but only in congratulatory terms. And then there is the strange anomaly, in the case of an old and successful mine, of the full Capital as a liability on one side of the balance-sheet, when it has all been returned, with good interest to boot, in the shape of dividends; and on the other side of the balance-sheet, to prop this up, the mine valued at scores of thousands of pounds —the original cost of it with buildings, plant, &c.—when it is practically worthless.

Depreciation.—The principles underlying depreciation are similar to those already spoken of under the second method of redeeming capital, for the amount written off for depreciation ought to accumulate as a reserve fund. Suppose it is estimated that a machine, or property of some kind, will last a certain number of years before renewal, the problem is, how much must be put by and invested each year of its life to redeem its cost. Sometimes the cost of repairs is considered as working or current expense, but perhaps more generally it is considered a capital charge and added to the prime cost. A more direct way would be to have the plant valued year by year, and to write it down each year to its estimated value, which would, of course, always be something above its removal value as long as it was any good on the mine. The usual method, however, is to write off a certain percentage depending on the character of the property considered—*e.g.*, $7\frac{1}{2}$† per cent. is often recommended for engines and waggons; and for horses, if they are considered as capital expenditure, 10 to 15 per cent. The following examples ‡ from the Rand are of interest:—For the year 1894 the Robinson Company wrote off 5 per cent. from all plant, buildings, &c., while the Worcester G. M. Company depreciated certain of their assets as follows:—

* *Op. cit.*, p. 55.
† See lectures by Messrs. Attlee and Evans before cited.
‡ Hatch and Chalmers, *Gold Mines of the Rand*, 1895, p. 270.

MINE ACCOUNTS.

Machinery, plant, and tools,	10 per cent.
Permanent works,	10 ,,
Buildings,	10 ,,
Permanent waterworks,	10 ,,
Live stock, carts, &c.,	5 ,,
Furniture,	5 ,,

The student may find an example in the annual report of almost every mining company. Many of these he may study with advantage.

The method of capriciously writing off for depreciation a lump sum one year and nothing during several other years is not to be recommended. When a good profit has resulted on a year's work, after a company has been passing through hard times, it is naturally felt that something must be done to put affairs in a sound financial condition, but this is better done by adding more largely to the reserve fund, and thus making it possible to write off a regular amount year by year for depreciation, than by treating depreciation irregularly, as something to be allowed for or not as convenient. For both depreciation and redemption of capital ought to be allowed for, even when a loss results on a year's work; otherwise, the loss is not recognised as being so great as it really is.

Reserve Fund.—The proper objects of the reserve fund have been stated* thus:—

(1) To equalise dividends.
(2) To meet accidental contingencies.
(3) To provide for sinking new shafts, buying new engines, &c.

The fund is, in fact, a sort of buffer between the Company and the sharp angularities of adverse circumstances. Should profits be small, it enables dividends to be continued; and should Capital expenditure be necessary, it relieves the shareholder from the necessity of putting his hand into his pocket. It is to be feared that the former object is rarely attained, the latter perhaps somewhat more often, though not so often as is desirable.

Although most balance-sheets show a reserve fund, it has in many, perhaps in most, cases no real existence; for it is evident that to be real it must be readily available—that is, invested in safe securities. A reserve fund is sometimes created by entering a large amount of what ought really to be "current expenditure" as "Capital expenditure," and so creating an artificial value for the assets. This may be illustrated simply thus:—

Capital and Liabilities.				Property and Assets.			
	£	s.	d.		£	s.	d.
Capital,	150,000	0	0	Property, &c.,	200,000	0	0
Reserve Fund,	50,000	0	0				
	200,000	0	0		200,000	0	0

Here it will be seen that the reserve fund is not available, and should it be the case that the assets ought to be written at a much less figure, the apparently large reserve would disappear.

BIBLIOGRAPHY.

The following references may be added to those already given in the text:—

* Armstrong and Harrison in discussion on Hoskold's paper. *Trans. Fed. Institute of Mining Engineers*, vol. iii., p. 739.

GENERAL CONSIDERATIONS AND COMPANIES' BOOKS.   III

Matheson; The Depreciation of Factories, 2nd Ed. London, 1893.
Dicksee; Comparative Depreciation Tables. London, 1895.
Guthrie; "Depreciation and Sinking Funds." *Accountant*, vol. ix. London, 1883. p. 437.
Murray; "Wear and Tear and Depreciation." *Accountant*, vol. xiii. London, 1887. p. 610.
Bogle; "Writing off of Depreciation of the Wasting Assets of a Joint Stock Company." *Trans. Chartered Accountants Students' Society of London*, 1889. p. 221.
Ladelle; "The Calculation of Depreciation." *Trans. Chartered Accountants Students' Society of London*, 1890. p. 114.
Walmsley; "Depreciation in Relation to Balance-Sheets." *Incorporated Accountants' Journal*, vol. v. London, 1893-94. p. 8.
Turner; "Depreciation of Machinery and Plant." *Accountants' Journal*, vol. xii. London, 1894-95. p. 49.

For matters relating to interest, annuities, and sinking funds, the "Institute of Actuaries' Textbook," Part I., by William Sutton, London, 1882, may be referred to. On pp. 156-163 there is given a list of the various interest and annuity tables which have been published.

CHAPTER XII.—GENERAL CONSIDERATIONS AND COMPANIES' BOOKS.

MINES may be owned and worked by private individuals, or by companies of persons associated together. The companies working mines are of three kinds, viz. :—

    Private partnership companies.
    Cost-book companies.
    Companies with liability limited by shares.

It is true that under the Companies' Act of 1862 (25 and 26 Vict. c. 89) there could exist two other kinds of companies—viz., companies with liability limited by guarantee, and registered companies with unlimited liability; but, as a matter of fact, such companies never exist in connection with mining enterprise, and therefore need not be considered here. We will consider the four cases, as far as accounts are affected, in the order—private individuals, private partnership companies, cost-book companies, limited liability companies.

Private Individuals.—When a mine is worked by an individual, so long as he keeps clear of bankruptcy, he can keep such accounts as he pleases, or neglect to keep any, and is accountable to no one. It is, however, reasonable to suppose that he wishes to work the mine profitably and honestly, making payments of monies owing by him in due season, and seeing that he is paid monies owing to him; to these ends, as pointed out in the introduction, a good system of accounts is necessary; further, should he become a bankrupt, he would be considered culpable if he had not kept a proper set of books.* Thus it is well, in every case, that the mine owner should have a complete system of accounts applicable to the nature of the operations he is engaged in, and that he should make a balance-sheet at regular intervals.

In making the balance-sheet the capital would not be a fixed amount, as it is in certain companies where it represents the amount subscribed by shareholders; but it would increase or diminish with the value of the mine and other assets, all of which should be carefully valued when the balance-sheet is made.

The owner is, of course, responsible for all liabilities incurred, and it may

* Williams, *Law and Practice in Bankruptcy*, 6th Ed. London, 1894, pp. 86, 90, and 91.

be mentioned that in distributing a bankrupt's estate priority is given to rates and taxes, "and also to what is due as wages or salaries to any of his clerks or servants, not exceeding £50, due in respect of services rendered during four months before the date of the receiving order; and also to what is due as wages to any labourer or workman, not exceeding £25, due in respect of services rendered during two months before the date of the receiving order."*

Private Partnership Companies.—These Companies can only exist legally for working mines when the number of partners is less than twenty. The partners may be bound together by a deed setting forth all the conditions of partnership, or may not; but in either case "It is one of the fundamental principles of partnership law, expressly recognised by the Partnership Act, 1890, that no person may be introduced as a partner without the consent of all existing partners."†

The necessity for a proper system of accounts in connection with a partnership business is thus pointed out by Lord-Justice Lindley. "If no books of accounts at all are kept, or if they are so kept as to be unintelligible, . . . and an account is directed by a court, every presumption will be made against those to whose negligence or misconduct the non-production of proper accounts is due."‡

A Capital Account is opened for every member of the firm, and "it is usual among mercantile men to treat all the accounts of a partnership as accounts of the firm, and to deal with the accounts of individual partners as if they were simply debtors or creditors of the firm."§

The following illustration is given by the eminent authority above quoted:—

Suppose A, B, C are partners, with a Capital of £3,000 subscribed by them equally; that they share profits and losses in proportion to their respective capitals, and that A has drawn out £500 and B has advanced £100. As the result of a year's working there are three possible cases:—

        Where there are no profits or losses.
        Where there is profit to be divided.
        Where there is loss to be made good.

We will set out only the second case; the student may refer to the work quoted for the others. Let the profit be £1,000; interest at 5 per cent. is charged on all sums brought in and taken out by each partner, and on his capital.

Dr.   1. PARTNERSHIP ACCOUNT.   *Cr.*

	£	s	d		£	s	d
To Stock,	3,000	0	0	By A's sum withdrawn, with interest for one year,	525	0	0
,, Interest on ditto for one year,	150	0	0				
,, B for advance, with interest for one year,	105	0	0				
,, Profit,	1,000	0	0	,, Balance,	3,730	0	0
	£4,255	0	0		£4,255	0	0

Dr.   2. A's ACCOUNT.   *Cr.*

	£	s	d		£	s	d
To sum withdrawn, with interest for one year,	525	0	0	By Capital,	1,000	0	0
,, Balance,	858	6	8	,, Interest on ditto,	50	0	0
				,, ⅓ share of profit,	333	6	8
	£1,383	6	8		£1,383	6	8

---

* Stephen, *New Commentaries on the Laws of England*, 12th Ed. 1895, vol. ii., p. 169.
† Lindley, *A Treatise on the Law of Partnership*, 6th Edit. 1893, London, p. 366.
‡ *Op. cit.*, p. 405.   § *Op. cit.*, p. 399.

GENERAL CONSIDERATIONS AND COMPANIES' BOOKS.

Dr.		3. B's Account.		Cr.
To Balance, . .	£1,488 6 8	By Capital, . . .	£1,000	0 0
		,, Interest on ditto, . .	50	0 0
		,, Advance and interest thereon, . . .	105	0 0
		,, ⅓ share of profits, . .	333	6 8
	£1,488 6 8		£1,488	6 8

Dr.		4. C's Account.		Cr.
To Balance,	£1,383 6 8	By Capital, . . .	£1,000	0 0
		,, Interest on ditto, . .	50	0 0
		,, ⅓ share of profits, . .	333	6 8
	£1,383 6 8		£1,383	6 8

Dr.		5. BALANCE-SHEET.		Cr.
To Balance as above, . .	£3,730 0 0	By Balance due as above to A,	£858	6 8
		,, ,, ,, B,	1,488	6 8
		,, ,, ,, C,	1,383	6 8
	£3,730 0 0		£3,730	0 0

It will be noticed that interest was allowed on Capital before the profit was estimated, which is the usual thing in a case of this kind.

Each partner is personally responsible for any debt incurred by the partnership, and in case of bankruptcy must hand over his private estate to a trustee. As in the case of private individuals (p. 112), certain salaries and wages are a preferential charge on the assets.

This class of company is not uncommon in Britain, and is also met with in the Colonies where several miners often combine to work a claim. The so-called "syndicates" are sometimes of this nature; though they are more often limited liability companies.

BIBLIOGRAPHY.

Lindley; A Treatise on the Law of Partnership, 6th Ed. London, 1893. pp. 939.

Smith, J. W.; The Law of Private Trading Partnerships. London, 1891. pp. 128. (A small hand-book).

Cost-Book Companies.—These companies, peculiar to mining enterprise, are only legal within the stannaries of Cornwall and Devon. They are of the nature of the common-law partnerships described in the last section; but the partners, or *adventurers* as they are called, may exceed twenty in number, and any one of them may transfer his interest to another person, without consent of the others. The liability of each partner is unlimited.

Cost-book Companies are regulated by the Stannaries Act, 1887, and by custom. They are subject to an ancient court, called the Stannary Court,* presided over by the Vice-Warden of the Stannaries. A set of rules may be agreed on and registered in the Stannary Court; or no rules may be made, in which case the concern must be conducted in accordance with the Stannaries Acts and established custom.

* Since the above was in type, the Stannary Court has been abolished by Act of Parliament (59 and 60 Vict., c. 45).

The Capital is not fixed in amount, but is subscribed by the adventurers as necessity arises.

Meetings of the adventurers must be held at least once in 16 weeks, and before every meeting the purser (secretary or manager) shall * "truly enter in the cost-book of the mine, accounts showing the actual financial position of the company at the end either of the financial month of such company last preceding the time of entry, or of the calendar month last preceding that time, including a statement of all credits, debts, and liabilities, and distinguishing in such accounts the amounts of calls paid, and calls not paid, and also all other accounts, documents, and things that the purser is required to enter therein by the custom of the stannaries, or by the direction of the company."

The cost-book is laid before each meeting of adventurers for examination, and if a profit has resulted on the 16 weeks' work a dividend is declared, while, on the other hand, if loss has occurred a call is made; thus the accounts are balanced and the books made ready for the records of the next period of work. After the meeting, the accounts must be printed and a copy sent to each shareholder. It has already been pointed out that a balance sheet is never made in connection with Cost-book Companies (see pp. 91, 135).

The term "cost-book," by definition in the Stannaries Act, "includes all books and papers relating to the business of a mine which are for the time being kept by a purser, or which, according to law or the custom of the stannaries, ought to be kept by him." But although the legal definition is so wide, there is a particular book kept at each mine which goes by this name (see p. 30). In it are first entered the rules, if such have been adopted; then before each pay-day the amounts of money due to the work-people and officials, and at the end of every 12 or 16 weeks, before the meetings of the adventurers :—

    A statement of ledger accounts.
    A list of all merchants' bills charged in the accounts.
    A list of shareholders.

Finally, at the meeting, the minutes are written in and the book is signed by the adventurers present.

Compared with "Limited" Companies the number of shares is relatively small, often about 6,000, and they can be easily transferred. It is simply necessary for the transferor to inform the purser that he hands over to the transferee certain of his shares, and for the transferee to inform the purser that he accepts those shares with their responsibilities. The transferee must then sign the cost-book, or ask the purser to do it for him if he cannot conveniently do it himself. The transaction may be accomplished by word of mouth, though it is now invariably done by writing, a sixpenny stamp rendering the deed legal.

The books connected with the recording of shareholders and the transfer of shares are :—
    Transfer Book.
    Share Ledger.
    Notices of Registration of Transfers Book.
    List of Shareholders.
    Guard Book for Deeds.

The transfers are first recorded in the transfer book, which is ruled thus :—

No.	From Whom.	To Whom.	Date of Transfer.	No. of Shares.	When Registered.

* Stannaries Act, 1887 (50 and 51 Vict. C. 43), Sec. 23.

GENERAL CONSIDERATIONS AND COMPANIES' BOOKS. 115

Then the transaction is recorded in the share ledger in its twofold aspect, the transferor being debited and the transferee being credited; this is called registering. The share ledger is ruled thus:—

895
Dr.   Cr.

Date of Transfer.	No. of Transfer.	To Whom Sold.	No. of Shares.	Date of Transfer.	No. of Transfer.	From Whom Purchased.	No. of Shares.

A numbered notice of registration is then sent to the transferee, and its counterfoil retained.

The list of shareholders is made up before every meeting, and shows at a glance any alterations in the number of shares held by each adventurer over a long period. It is ruled thus:—

Name.	Date of Meeting.	Date of Meeting.	Date of Meeting.	Date of Meeting.	Date of Meeting.	Date of Meeting.	Date of Meeting.	Date of Meeting.	Date of Meeting.	Date of Meeting.

Opposite the name of each shareholder is written the number of shares held by him at the date of each meeting.

Dividends paid are recorded in a list, but a ledger is used for keeping an account of the payment of calls.

If a shareholder wishes to sever his connection with a Cost-book Company, and can neither sell his shares, nor induce anyone to accept them as a gift, he may relinquish them, provided that he pays his share of the liabilities up to the time of relinquishment *minus* his share of the assets, and that the Company does not stop the mine within the six weeks following the relinquishment.

Wages, not exceeding those due for three months, are a first charge upon all assets of the company.*

The cost-book principle, although little known outside Cornwall and Devon before 1840, dates back to a very early time in the stannaries. Since 1862 its merits have often been compared with those of the limited liability system. Some of the advantages it possesses are:—

1. There is no expense in starting a cost-book company, as against cost of promotion, underwriting shares, &c., generally necessary in the case of a limited liability company.

2. The Capital is unlimited, just as much being called up from time to time as is necessary to test a property thoroughly, or to bring a mine into a profitable condition. In the other system the Capital is fixed in amount, and may prove insufficient, and although there is the remedy of issuing debentures, or of reconstruction, yet the first may be difficult to arrange, and the latter is always a very undesirable step.

3. The frequent meetings are an advantage in that the adventurers have frequent news of the mine, and meet together to discuss the position of the venture and to balance the accounts. Further, the direction and control of the company are vested in the body of shareholders and not in directors. But there is, however, an inevitable tendency to pay every penny of profit as a

* Stannaries Act, 1887, Sec. 4.

dividend and to delay making calls, so that improvements are put off from meeting to meeting, and expensive methods of working, and inadequate and antiquated machinery and appliances are often continued in operation long after the time when, in the best interests of the mine, they ought to have been replaced.

The unlimited liability is especially objectionable to adventurers who live outside the stannaries, for though they may be prepared to lose the price of the shares they buy, they do not wish to be liable for an unknown amount, which, in a properly conducted concern, would never be much; but which has, through mismanagement or other causes, in some cases proved very considerable on a winding-up of affairs. Therefore although the principle has answered very well in the past, and has much to recommend it when the adventurers live near a mine, yet it has not proved satisfactory where the general public is appealed to for Capital; and for that reason it seems to be dying a natural death.

BIBLIOGRAPHY.

Collier; A Treatise on the Law Relating to Mines. London, 1849.
English; Mining Almanack. London, 1849, p. 237.
Higgins; The Gold Companies and the Cost-Book System. London, 1853.
Tapping; The Cost Book: its Principles and Practice. London, 1854.
—— The Principles of the Cost-Book System Practically Considered. London, 1867.
Batten; The Stannaries Act, 1869. Edited with notes. London, 1873.
Williams; "Cornish Mining and the Cost-Book Principle," *Accountant*, vol. xvii., 1891, p. 246.

Also, Manson, pp. 366-376; T. Eustace Smith, pp. 3 and 4; and some of the books on the law of companies mentioned on p. 121.

The *Mining Journal* contains many articles and numerous letters on the Cost-Book System.

Limited Liability Companies.—Mines dependent upon British capital are generally worked by companies of this class. Their chief characteristic is that the liability per share is limited to the nominal amount of such share. Limited liability companies are regulated by numerous Acts of Parliament, the earliest now in force, and the principal one, being the Companies Act, 1862. Somewhat similar Acts have been passed in other countries.*

A limited liability company must consist of at least seven members, each holding not less than one share; and it must be registered at the Joint Stock Companies' Registration Office, which, for England, is Somerset House. In registering, it is necessary to present a "Memorandum of Association," subscribed to by at least seven members of the company. This memorandum must contain:—†

1. The Name of the proposed Company, with the addition of the word "Limited" as the last word in such name:
2. The part of the United Kingdom, whether *England*, *Scotland*, or *Ireland*, in which the registered office of the Company is proposed to be situate:
3. The Objects for which the proposed Company is to be established:
4. A Declaration that the liability of the members is limited:
5. The Amount of Capital with which the Company proposes to be regis-

---

* Thus some of the "limited companies" working mines in the Transvaal are registered under the Limited Liability Act of the South African Republic.
† Companies Act, 1862 (25 and 26 Vict. c. 89, sec. 8).

tered, divided into shares of a certain fixed amount, subject to the following Regulations :
(1.) That no Subscriber shall take less than One Share :
(2.) That each Subscriber of the Memorandum of Association shall write opposite to his Name the Number of Shares he takes.

In addition to the Memorandum of Association, Companies generally have Articles of Association. These may be registered contemporaneously with the Company, or they may be adopted at any subsequent time by special resolution. *"The Articles are the internal regulations of the Company, and play a subsidiary part to the Memorandum. They define the duties, rights, and powers of the governing body as between themselves and the Company at large, and the mode and form in which changes in the internal regulations of the Company may from time to time be made. . . . The Articles define also the manner in which the various powers of the Company are to be exercised." The Memorandum is fixed and unalterable, but the Articles can be amended by special resolution.

The interests of the shareholders and the management of the concerns of the Company are entrusted to a Board of "Directors," which appoints the necessary officials.

The accounts of the Company must be audited at least once a year; the first auditors being appointed by the directors, and subsequent auditors by the Company in general meeting. An auditor "is appointed in the interests of the shareholders alone. . . . He owes no duties to the directors."†

The Capital of a limited liability company may consist of stocks or shares, and debentures.

Stocks.—The differences between stocks and shares are :—1. The latter may be partially paid up, but the former must be fully paid. 2. Nothing less than one whole share can be sold, but a fractional part of stock may be disposed of. Fully-paid shares may be converted into stocks.

Shares.—These are of several kinds, the commonest being preference, ordinary, and founders'. Preference shares have a prior claim to interest, in case a profit has to be divided, according to conditions laid down when they were issued ; but if sufficient profit is not made to pay interest on the preference shares, such deficit does not rank as a liability of the Company, as does the interest on debentures. Preference shares are, however, often issued with cumulative dividends, which means that if in a bad year a full preference dividend is not paid, the amount left unpaid will be a first charge on future profits after debenture interest. Founders' shares are generally few in number, and carry exceptional possibilities. They are sometimes arranged so that after the ordinary shares have received a certain interest, say 10 per cent., the founders' shares take a half, or other proportion, of the remaining profit. So that, should a Company be very successful, they become of great value, to the detriment of the ordinary shares. Nowadays, they are not regarded with much favour, and are very rarely met with in connection with Mining Companies.

Stocks and shares may be acquired in three ways ; a shareholder may have been a subscriber to the Memorandum of Association, or he may have had his shares allotted to him, or he may have purchased them. Each share has a distinctive number, which is not the case with the shares of a cost-book company. Share-certificates, printed from an engraved plate, are issued to each shareholder; they carry his name, the number of shares he holds, and the numbers of the shares. Share-warrants, though only issued in respect to fully-paid shares, which are thus converted into stocks, are, however, used to some extent. A warrant states that its holder is the pro-

---

* Hurrell and Hyde, *The Joint Stock Companies Practical Guide* ; London, 1889, p. 14.
† Hurrell and Hyde, *Op. cit.*, p. 58.

prietor of a certain number of shares, and it must carry a stamp of a value equal to 1⅛ per cent. on the amount of the shares. The stocks it represents are transferred by the mere passing from hand to hand of the warrant; whereas shares for which only a certificate has been issued must be transferred by a deed carrying an *ad valorem* stamp.

Debentures.—These may be issued when the company commences, or subsequently, when it is wished to borrow money for development or other purpose; in either case the company pledges the whole or a part of its assets as security for the payment of the principal and interest on the debentures. In fact, debentures are of the nature of an ordinary mortgage; but, as the sum borrowed is generally large, it would be difficult to get it from a single individual or firm, and so it is obtained from a large number of small lenders, the property being mortgaged to certain trustees in favour of the debenture holders. Debentures are also sometimes created and issued to shareholders in lieu of interest, the shareholders' consent being first obtained.

In reference to book-keeping, the Companies Act, 1862, makes various provisions, the chief being as follow:—

A. * " The directors shall cause true accounts to be kept—
"Of the stock in trade † of the company;
"Of the sums of money received and expended by the company, and the matter in respect of which such receipt and expenditure takes place; and
"Of the credits and liabilities of the company."

It will be seen that, as far as these regulations concern mining companies, the information required is all contained in the books and forms described in the early chapters of this manual.

B. ‡ Once at the least in every year the directors shall lay before the company in general meeting a statement of the income and expenditure for the past year, made up to a date not more than three months before such meeting.

"The statement so made shall show, arranged under the most convenient heads, the amount of gross income, distinguishing the several sources from which it has been derived, and the amount of gross expenditure, distinguishing the expenses of the establishment, salaries, and other like matters. Every item of expenditure fairly chargeable against the year's income shall be brought into account so that a just balance of profit and loss may be laid before the meeting, and in cases where any item of expenditure which may in fairness be distributed over several years has been incurred in any one year, the whole amount of such item shall be stated, with the addition of the reasons why only a portion of such expenditure is charged against the income of the year."

The above two paragraphs refer to the revenue or profit and loss account which has already been spoken of (see p. 86).

C. Table A, sec. 81, refers to the balance sheet.

D. Sec. 25 of the Act provides that a register of shareholders shall be kept containing:—

(1) The names and addresses, and the occupations, if any, of the members of the company, with the addition, in the case of a company having a Capital divided into Shares, of a Statement of the Shares held by each member, distinguishing each Share by its Number; and of the amount paid, or agreed to be considered as paid, on the shares of each member.

(2) The date at which the Name of any Person was entered in the Register as a member.

* Table A, sec. 78. † *i.e.*, assets.
‡ Table A, sec. 79 and 80. It is customary, however, to expunge Table A by Articles of Association, or at any rate the greater portion of it.

GENERAL CONSIDERATIONS AND COMPANIES' BOOKS.   119

(3) The date at which any person ceased to be a member.
This register may take the form of a list, or the share-ledger alone may be kept as answering the requirements of the Act.

The share-ledger may be ruled in many ways.* The following example is illustrative :—

Name........................   Address......................
Description........................
Date of entry as a Member...............   Ceased to be a Member...............

Date.	No. of Transfer.	Transferor or Transferee.	Folio.	Distinctive Numbers.				Cr.	Dr.	Balance.	Amount.
				Acquired.		Transferred.					
				From	To	From	To				

The Register of Members is, under certain conditions, open to inspection, and copies may be had at the rate of 6d. per hundred words.†

E. According to Sec. 26 an annual return must be made to the Registrar of Joint-Stock Companies containing a list of members and particulars of the capital of the Company. The form of this return was altered from that given in the Act by notice in the *London Gazette* of the 14th day of April, 1885.

F. Sec. 43 provides that a Register of all Mortgages and Charges specifically affecting the property of the Company shall be kept.

G. It is necessary to keep ‡ "Minutes of all Resolutions and Proceedings of General Meetings of the Company, and of the Directors or Managers of the Company in cases where there are Directors and Managers. Two minute books are usually kept, one for the minutes of Directors' meetings, and the other for those of general meetings.

Of Company books not previously discussed, brief mention will be made under the two heads—(1) Books connected with Shares; (2) Miscellaneous Books.

Books Connected with Shares.—The **Allotment Book** contains, in tabular form, an account of the number of shares allotted to each member, with the distinctive numbers of the shares. It may also provide for a record of the payment of the several instalments on the shares, if they are paid for by instalments.

The **Transfer Receipt Book** contains forms with counterfoils for acknowledging the receipt of transfer deeds, a note being appended at the bottom saying when the new share-certificate will be ready. The old share-certificate must be given in with the transfer deed, and is retained at the company's office.

In the case where the transferor has sold shares to a number of different persons, as each transferee cannot have a certificate to attach to the transfer deed which he, or his agent, hands in at the office of the company, therefore the transferor deposits the original certificate of his shares with the company, and the secretary of the company certifies on each transfer deed that the certificate

---
* See Carter, *Practical Book-Keeping*. 6th Ed., 1890, p. 53. Cummins, *Guide to the Formation of the Accounts of Limited Liability Companies*, 1895, p. 22. Fitzpatrick and Fowke, *Secretary's Manual*, 1895, p. 54.
† Sec. 32.   ‡ Sec. 67.

of the shares indicated on the deed has been so deposited. This is called **certification.** Should the transferor possess more shares than he transfers, a new certificate is issued to him for the residue.

List of Transfers.—When the transfers are received for registration, they are dated and numbered consecutively, after which they are entered in a book which may be ruled thus—

No. of Transfer.	Name of Transferor.	Distinctive Numbers.		No. of Shares Transferred.	Initials of Directors.	Name of Transferee.	Address.	Memorandum.
		From	To					

The transfers are then brought before the Directors who are responsible for them. They are examined and initialled by the Directors, and the book may also be initialled in the column provided for that purpose.

Share-Certificate Book.—This contains forms of share certificates with counterfoils. The certificate is written from the transfer and then examined by the Directors, who again initial the transfer and the counterfoil of the share-certificate. When the new share-certificates are handed over, a receipt is obtained; sometimes the form of receipt is on the counterfoil, or it may be attached to the certificate from which it can be torn off, or it may be a separate form.*

Guard Book for Transfers.—In this the transfer deeds are pasted consecutively for preservation and ease of reference.

Miscellaneous Books.

Agenda Book. In this are written the matters of business to be brought before the Directors at a board meeting.

Directors' Attendance Book, is signed by each Director when present at a meeting.

Guard Book, for all printed matter, forms, &c., connected with the business of the company.

Guard Book, for all press cuttings commenting on the company or its property.

Register of Documents.

Seal Book, for containing an account of the documents to which the company's seal has been affixed. This is not always kept, for the seal can only be affixed to a document with the authority of the Directors, and the fact of this having been given would be noted in the minutes of Directors' meetings.

BIBLIOGRAPHY.
LEGAL.

Buckley; Law and Practice under the Companies' Acts. 6th ed. London, 1891. pp. 805.

Emden; Winding-up Companies. 4th ed. London, 1891. pp. 1034.

---

* For full details of the books and forms above briefly mentioned—and for many other necessary forms, such as those connected with allotment, calls, &c.—the student is referred to *The Company Secretary*, by W. H. Fox, London, 1895; or the *Secretary's Manual*, by Fitzpatrick & Fowke, London, 1897.

GENERAL CONSIDERATIONS AND COMPANIES' BOOKS. 121

Fowke; The Companies' Acts, 1862 to 1890. London, 1893. pp. 403. A reprint of the Acts.
Gore-Browne ; Concise Precedents under the Companies' Acts, 1862 to 1890. London, 1892. pp. 548.
Hamilton and Metcalfe ; A Manual of Company Law. London, 1891. pp. 468.
Healey, Wheeler, and Burney ; A Treatise on the Law and Practice relating to Joint-Stock Companies. 3rd ed. London, 1894. pp. 1246.
Mackenzie, Geare, and Hamilton ; Company Law. London, 1893.
Manson ; Law of Trading and other Companies. 2nd ed. London, 1893. pp. 966.
Palmer ; Company Precedents. 6th ed. Part I. London, 1895. pp. 1143. Part II. 1896.
Palmer ; Shareholders', Directors', and Voluntary Liquidators' Legal Companion. 14th ed. London, 1894. pp. 231.
Smith, T. Eustace ; A Summary of the Law of Companies. 5th ed. London, 1891. pp. 342. A Student's Manual.
Smith, J. W. ; The Law of Joint-Stock Companies. 23rd thousand. London, 1894. pp. 202. A small Handbook.
Thring and Rendel ; The Law and Practice of Joint-Stock and other Companies. 5th ed. London, 1889. pp. 664.

GENERAL.

Brown ; Secretaries of Public Companies and their Duties. 2nd ed. London (about 1893). pp. 78.
Cummins ; Guide to the Formation of the Accounts of Limited Liability Companies. London, 1894. pp. 48.
Ennis and Ennis ; The Registration of Transfers of Transferable Stocks, Shares and Securities. London, 1893. pp. 128.
Fitzpatrick and Fowke ; The Secretary's Manual of the Law and Practice of Joint-Stock Companies. 4th ed. London, 1897.
Fox ; The Company Secretary. London, 1895. pp. about 250.
Hurrell and Hyde; The Joint-Stock Companies Practical Guide. London, 1890. pp. 266.
Jordan and Gore-Browne ; Handy Book on the Formation. Management and Winding-up of Joint-Stock Companies. 18th ed. London, 1895. pp. 350.
Manson ; Debentures. London, 1894. pp. 248.
Palgrave ; The Chairman's Handbook. 9th ed. London (about 1894). pp. 110.
Pixley ; The Shareholder's Handbook. 2nd ed. London, 1886. pp. 94.
  ,,   The Director's Handbook. 2nd ed. London, 1890. pp. 116.

PART V.

REPORTS AND STATISTICS.

This section is divided into the following three chapters :—
  XIII. Reports of Inspections of Workings and Machinery.
  XIV. Periodical and Special Reports of Mining Companies.
  XV. Mining Statistics.

CHAPTER XIII.—REPORTS OF INSPECTIONS OF WORKINGS AND MACHINERY.

THE Coal Mines Regulation Act, 1887, requires that certain reports shall be made in connection with the safety of workmen. At collieries, they are practically limited to this subject. Inspections are also made regularly at mines under the Metalliferous Mines Act, and reports are frequently made, relating not only to the safety of the workmen, but also to the richness or poverty of the working places, and any other points of interest which may develop from day to day. Although written reports are not necessitated by the Metalliferous Mines Regulation Act, 1872, itself, they may be made obligatory by the Special Rules. They are useful for reference, also, as probably securing more efficient inspection, and as evidence in cases under the Employers Liability Act.

The following subdivision will be made :—
  A. Books used at mines under the Coal Mines Act.
  B. Books used at mines under the Metalliferous Mines Act.
  C. Books in general use.

A. Inspections.—It is provided in General Rule 4, Sec. 49, of the Coal Mines Regulation Act, 1887,* that there shall be an inspection of the underground workings by a competent person before the workmen enter the mine, and that "a report specifying where noxious or inflammable gas (if any) was found present, and what defects (if any) in roofs or sides, and what (if any) other source of danger were or was observed, shall be recorded without delay in a book to be kept at the mine for the purpose, and accessible to the workmen, and such report shall be signed by, and so far as the same does not consist of printed matter, shall be in the handwriting of the person who made the inspection."

Inspections must also be made in the course of each shift, but these need not be recorded, unless the mine be worked continuously throughout the

---
* This Act refers to mines of coal, stratified ironstone, shale, and fireclay. See also Coal Mines Regulation Act, 1896 (59 and 60 Vict., c. 43), Sec. 5 (1).

twenty-four hours, when one such inspection must be recorded each day. Each of these inspections is, however, often recorded.

A daily report on the ventilation is frequently made, although not required by the Act.

Rule 5, Sec. 49, of the Act requires that a daily inspection shall be made of the external parts of the machinery, guides and conductors in the shafts, headgears, ropes, chains, and other similar appliances of the mine which are in actual use both above ground and below ground; and that a weekly inspection shall be made of the state of the shafts by which persons ascend or descend. A report of such inspections must be recorded without delay in a book to be kept at the mine for the purpose, and every such report shall be signed by the person who made it. A thorough overhauling of winding ropes is generally done once a week, as it is scarcely possible to do this every day.

Rule 7 provides that if it is found that a mine or any part of it is dangerous, it must be specially examined, and the report of such examination recorded in a book kept for the purpose.

Lastly, Rule 38 allows the workmen to appoint two of their number, or other two practical working miners, to inspect the mine from time to time. Such inspection must be reported, and the report recorded in a book kept for the purpose, and should danger be noted, a copy of the report must be sent to H.M. Inspector of Mines for the district in which the mine is situated.

The various inspections mentioned above may be summarised—

Underground,	{ Inspections before commencing work, { Inspections during work,	
Surface and Underground,	{ Inspections of Machinery, Ropes, Headgear, &c.,	Daily.
	Inspections of Shafts and Ropes,	Weekly.
Underground,	{ Inspections of dangerous places, { Inspections on behalf of workmen,	As necessary. "From time to time."

Report Books.—For recording the reports of these various inspections, manuscript books alone are sufficient; but as the reports must be written without delay, the books get very dirty. At one colliery, in order to obviate this, and to enable the report to be read at once by anyone interested, it is written on a slip of paper, with printed headings, provided for the purpose; the slip is then sent to the surface and the report copied into a book by a clerk. When the official who made the inspection comes to the surface, he signs the copy after examining it. The original report is also kept.

The Act, however, provides that any report "may be partly in print (including lithograph) and partly in writing." The advantages of a printed form are that the report can be more easily read; the patience of the official reporting, who is probably not an expert penman, is spared; and the report books are kept clean and tidy.

There is no need that each of the seven inspections should be in a separate book. If a moderate-sized volume is provided, forms can be printed on each page for recording each of the daily inspections, so that one opening of the book shows all the reports of the daily inspections for two days, and sufficient space may be left at the bottom to write the weekly reports on the day the examination is made. More than three forms might be necessary to record the daily inspections, as the number would depend on the number of persons reporting—*e.g.*, one deputy might report on one district underground, and another deputy on another district, and so on; separate forms would have to be provided for each deputy. But no difficulty would present itself in designing a report book applicable to any particular colliery.

Mr. Maskell W. Peace, in his work on the Coal Mines Regulation Act, 1887, suggests various forms * for the reports of the inspections necessary under the Act.

Mr. Hutchings † also publishes a useful set of forms for recording inspections. The following is one of his forms for the daily underground inspection :—

COAL MINES REGULATION ACT, 1887.

.... Mine. .... District.

I, the undersigned, being a person duly appointed for that purpose, as required by General Rule No. 4, hereby declare that I have carefully inspected all the working places of the above-named District and all the roadways leading thereto ; and that I find the same to be in the condition hereinafter stated, namely :—

Presence of Gas,...

Ventilation,..

State of Roof and Sides,..

General Safety,...

Dated this   day of   , 189 , at   o'clock in the
                                    Signed..

The next form, for the daily inspection of machinery, is one of the set ‡ published by Messrs. John Steen & Co. of Wolverhampton.

REPORT OF INSPECTION OF MACHINERY.

.............................Colliery.   Pit No........................   District.........................
At................o'clock. 189
                                                        50 & 51 Vic., cap. 58, Sec. 10.

I (or we), the undersigned, have carefully inspected (according to General Rule 5), at this mine.....................Ground, and have to report that the

External parts of ⎫
  Machinery are ⎭
Guides and Conductors
Head Gear
Ropes
Chains
Other appliances
Remarks
  Signature of   ⎫ ....
  Competent Person ⎭

Measurement of Ventilating Current.—The Coal Mines Regulation Act, 1887, provides that "In the case of mines required by this Act to be under the control of a certificated manager, § the quantity of air in the respective splits or currents shall at least once in every month be measured and entered in a book to be kept for the purpose at the mine."

It is not unusual for these measurements to be made every week, and it is well to record the actual data obtained, in addition to the quantity of air

---

* Peace, *The Coal Mines Regulation Act*, 1887. London, 1888, pp. 253-271. See also Bulman and Redmayne, *Colliery Working and Management*. London, 1896, pp. 64-73.

† Hutton Street, Whitefriars, London.

‡ *Catalogue of Registers, Report Books, &c., for use in Collieries*, Compiled by W. J. Davies. Wolverhampton.

§ *i.e.*, those mines in which more than 30 persons are employed (Sec. 20).

REPORTS OF INSPECTIONS OF WORKINGS AND MACHINERY. 125

calculated; columns can readily be ruled in a book for this purpose or a printed form can be used. Here is an example :—

Date.	Where Measured.	Water Gauge.	Velocity.		Velocity in feet per minute.	Sectional Area of Airway.	Quantity of air in feet per minute.	Remarks.	Signature.
			Time in Minutes.	Anemometer Readings.					

Columns may also be provided for recording the height of barometer, state of weather, and humidity of air, if thought desirable.

On or before the 21st of January every year, particulars of the ventilation at each colliery must be sent to the Inspector of Mines of the district in which a colliery is situated. Official forms for these returns have been issued. It is well to keep a copy of each return on duplicates bound in book form, or to have counterfoils attached to the returns and to bind the forms together.

Permits to Fire Shots and Carry a Safety-Lamp Key.—The firing of shots in collieries may often be very dangerous unless carried on with proper precautions, and it may only be done by properly authorised persons; so also proper authority is required in order that any person may unlock safety lamps underground, for the purpose of relighting them. It is best that the "permits" should be given on printed forms; the forms being bound together with counterfoils, so that a record of all permits given may be kept. Provision may be made on the counterfoil for a receipt to be signed by the person to whom the permit is given.

Three forms are often used, one with authority to blast only, a second with authority to carry a safety-lamp key only, and a third with authority both to blast and to carry a safety-lamp key.

B. The following inspections are made and reported at a metalliferous mine in the North of England. The underground workings are examined every shift, that is three times a day as there are three shifts; and reports as to the safety and value of the various working places are written by the agents as soon as they return to the surface.

Each engineman makes a careful examination of his engine every shift as soon after he takes charge of it as possible. The result of this inspection he records in a diary provided for the purpose. The ropeman, a quondam sailor, examines the winding ropes, chains, and cages daily during lunch-time, and once a week he thoroughly overhauls the ropes. The engineer examines the other machinery at frequent intervals. The pumpmen climb through the shafts daily and examine the pumps; and once a week the shafts are examined carefully from top to bottom.

The boilers are thoroughly examined every time they are cleansed, and a record is made of their condition.

The following is a form of "boiler book" used at a mine in Cornwall :—

Date of Cleansing.	Name of Engine.	No. of Boiler.	Remarks.	By Whom Cleansed.

At a mine on the Rand, books are kept for recording the following inspections:—

Once a week, each wire hauling-rope is carefully inspected by the engineer and pitman, the results of such inspection being carefully noted—each signing the report.

The boilers are looked at each day, and thoroughly inspected each time they are cleansed, which is done monthly.

The engines are inspected daily by the engineer.

A daily inspection is also made of the shafts and skip-roads by the pitman.

A careful account is kept of the estimated value of the various ends and other places of interest, the reef being measured and samples taken. Here is one form of record used:—

ASSAY BOOK.

Date.	Sample from	Width of Reef.		Width of Quartzite.		Amalgamation Method per ton of 2,000 lbs.			Fusion Method per ton of 2,000 lbs.			Mark of Sample.	Name of Reef.	Remarks.
		Ft.	Ins.	Ft.	Ins.	oz.	dwts.	grs.	oz.	dwts.	grs.			

C. In sinking shafts, whatever their purpose may be, careful records should always be kept of the character of the rocks passed through at various depths. Such a record would often be of value for subsequent reference, and is always of great general interest.

The following is a form in use for reporting the progress of boreholes:—

REPORT OF BORING.

At..

Week ending........................*189*

Depth Bored.*		Total Depth Bored.†		Nature of Strata.	Remarks.
Feet.	Inches.	Feet.	Inches.		

The next is a form for the permanent record of a borehole:—

RECORD OF BOREHOLE No.........

Put down at.....................

Date.	Depth to Change of Rock.	Nature of Rock.	Thickness of each Variety of Rock.	Remarks.

The exact position of the borehole must be marked on a plan or map.

Both the Mines Regulation Acts, and also the Factory and Workshop Acts,

* *i.e.*, Increase in depth.   † *i.e.*, Total depth from the surface.

provide that notices of accidents to persons employed must be sent to the Inspector of the district. Official forms for these notices are published, and it is convenient, as in the case of other official forms, to have them bound up in book form, with duplicates or counterfoils, so that a permanent record of accidents may be kept. A register of accidents is imperative in the case of the surface-works of mines under the Metalliferous Act, as they are governed by the Factory and Workshop Acts.

CHAPTER XIV.—REPORTS OF MINING COMPANIES.

SECTION 49 of the Companies Act, 1862, prescribes that "A General Meeting of every Company under this Act shall be held once at the least in every year"; and in Table A it is provided that a yearly profit and loss account, the balance sheet, as also the auditors' report on the balance sheet and accounts, shall be laid before the Company in general meeting; and, further, that a printed copy of the balance sheet shall, seven days previously to such meeting, be served on every member. Thus, the Act provides that a profit and loss account, balance sheet, and auditors' report shall be set before the shareholders each year. In addition, however, Directors generally issue a printed report, consisting of tabular statements and explanatory text, often with one or more diagrams in order to make it more clearly understood.

The object of the Directors, in making these reports, is, or ought to be, to give as full an explanation as possible of the position of the Company with regard to the past, present, and future. The past, as it explains the present, and as the experience it has yielded bears upon the future; the present, in relation to the financial position of the Company and the state of the mine; the future, as to its prospects.

Reports ought to be absolutely honest. It is impossible to imagine circumstances under which it would be best to deceive the shareholders either by assertion or omission. Shareholders expect risk in mining enterprises, and, given Directors who deal perfectly openly with them, they are prepared to support all that is reasonably and honestly undertaken.

To some extent shareholders are protected with regard to the financial part of a report by the statutory examination of the accounts by auditors; but with regard to the part which describes the condition and prospects of the mine, and which is often the most important part, they are entirely dependent on the officials.

There is no doubt that it is very difficult for an official to put himself into a sufficiently judicial frame of mind to write a report which gives to the shareholders a correct impression of the condition of the mine; there is always the temptation for him to write rather what he thinks and hopes than what he has actually seen, or logically deduced. Further there is the difficulty of explaining to the shareholders precisely what he intends; as he is in daily touch with the mine, everything about it is so familiar, that he can rarely help assuming too much knowledge on the part of those for whose benefit he is writing; he cannot, without great effort, bring himself down to the level of those who know nothing about the mine, and little, if anything, about mining in general; nor is it easy for him to describe the state of his mine without using technical terms, which are as Greek to the multitude.

It is very important that a report should be prepared, not solely with the view of producing a business-like or artistic pamphlet which will excite the admiration of accountants or mining engineers, but so that those who are versed

MINE ACCOUNTS.

neither in accountancy nor mining engineering can form a just estimate of the position of the Company. The Directors appeal to the general public, not to experts, for financial support, and therefore it is only fair that they should present a report, a sufficient part of which, set out in simple language entirely free from technicalities, can be grasped by any one.

A good annual or half-yearly report, carefully compiled, is not only of great value and interest to the shareholders of a Company, but its preparation is a most valuable exercise to the Manager and Directors. The time and data necessary for carefully weighing and estimating a Company's position from all points of view cannot be obtained at weekly or monthly intervals; if, however, it be done thoroughly every six months, or even annually, benefit must accrue to the undertaking.

Mining enterprises will always be speculative, though in very varying degrees; nevertheless, it will be generally allowed that it is desirable to reduce this element to a minimum, and complete and accurate reports certainly tend in that direction.

Proceeding to consider reports more in detail, we may observe, in passing, that the prospectus of a Company may be looked upon as its first report, save that it has no past to deal with, and speaks chiefly of the future; it also has a special object, namely, to induce the public to subscribe capital. Although it is almost impossible to avoid a little high colouring, yet *"those who issue a prospectus holding out to the public the great advantages which will accrue to persons who will take shares in a proposed undertaking, and inviting them to take shares on the faith of the representations therein contained, are bound to state everything with strict and scrupulous accuracy, and not only to abstain from stating as fact that which is not so, but to omit no one fact within their knowledge, the existence of which might in any degree affect the nature, or extent, or quality of the privileges and advantages which the prospectus holds out as inducements to take shares."

The annual or half-yearly report of mining companies, in its simplest form, consists of—

    Directors' Report.
    Manager's Report.
    Profit and Loss Account.
    Balance Sheet.

Sometimes, however, it is a much more elaborate affair, containing, in addition, the underground manager's report; or, where a Company has several mines or establishments, a number of reports, one from each of the various chiefs; also numerous tabular statements, which may be classified under the heads—

  1. Historical.
  2. Ledger Accounts.
  3. Analyses of Cost and Expenditure. } For period considered.
  4. Ore treated, and results.

1. These are tables showing how the share capital has arrived at its present condition by sub-divisions of shares, new issues, and so on; the amount of ore treated in past years, and the results obtained; also the costs of machinery and of working, and the dividends paid.

2. In addition to the profit and loss account, other ledger accounts are sometimes published, such as the account of the saleable product obtained, receipts and expenditure account, and especially one or more working accounts, if such be kept.

* Buckley, *Law and Practice under the Companies' Acts*, 6th ed., London, 1891, p. 107.

Plans and diagrams are often appended to add clearness to reports.
We will now consider the various parts of a report of a mining company in the order—managers' reports, diagrams, tabular statements, and directors' report.

Managers' Reports.—As a rule there is no need to publish more than one of these reports, for two or more generally lead to much repetition and lack of uniformity, and occasionally even to confusion; besides making it much more laborious for a reader to get at the true position of affairs. In the 20th half-yearly report of a certain large silver mining and smelting company there are four managers' reports, viz. :—

> General Manager's Report.
> Mining Manager's Report.
> Chief Metallurgist's Report.
> Report of Manager of Subsidiary Metallurgical Works.

The General Manager's Report contains much of the information given in the others, but it is for the half-year only, while the other three are for the whole year; the reports of the two metallurgists differ from each other in that one gives data and tables for the two half-years separately, while the other gives those for the whole year; other points might be noticed, but sufficient has been said to show a lack of uniformity which might be confusing, unless great care were exercised in reading, and which certainly makes the time and energy necessary to get at the bearing of the whole report much greater than need be; it would have been better if the general manager had taken the other three reports and woven them into a harmonious whole, amplifying and condensing as he thought necessary. The natural sequence in such matters is that the subordinates of each department report to their superior officer, the head of each department reports to the general manager, who —having all these reports before him, and in addition his own personal knowledge—writes a comprehensive report to the Directors illustrated with diagrams if possible.

A somewhat difficult matter is to decide what ground a report should cover. It is quite unnecessary to give a complete description of the property, and to describe the character of the mineral deposits and every point of interest in every report, but this may be done at intervals. Thus the second annual report of De Beers Consolidated Mines, Ltd., published in 1891, contains a complete description of the mines and method of working, of the plant and methods of treating the "blue ground" at the surface; there is evidently no need to repeat this every year.

When no general description of the deposits on a property has been given, it is evidently useless to speak in detail of this lode and that lode, of this level or that end, as it is quite impossible for the shareholders to picture in their minds the position or relation of these various points; and consequently the fragmentary allusions have no meaning to them. However, when once a comprehensive description has been given, the general manager may assume that the shareholder has it before him, and may write his report accordingly until the description gets out of date, or becomes inapplicable for some reason; a new description should then be published.

A time when a special report can be published with great propriety is at the end of the first period in the history of the mine; that is when the engines, dressing plant, and other surface arrangements have been completed, the shafts sunk and, generally, the mine got into good working order. In the case of a colliery where deep shafts have been sunk, a history of the sinking is both interesting and instructive; this may be presented graphically, as, for instance, by a diagram in which the ordinates represent time, and the abscissæ

9

the depths attained. Any hindrances there may have been in sinking, at once strike the eye on such a diagram, and explanatory notes may be added at such points. A similar diagram may be used to show the water met with at various depths. Particular circumstances may suggest other diagrams.

The future prospects of a mine are very rarely adequately treated in mining reports. The manager generally satisfies himself with vague references, often, it is to be feared, written down without a very careful estimation and correlation of facts; yet frequently a numerical estimate of some value could be arrived at by careful measurement * and calculation. Such estimates are accepted as of some value, when a company is formed to take over a mine as a going concern, though they are often of the nature of special pleading; surely they might be made of value as definite information for the shareholders when undertaken regularly, as a part of his ordinary duty, by the manager of a mine.

The manager's report should contain references to the workmen, their health, wages earned, accidents, and any other points that might be of interest in this connection. Without appealing to any higher motive, it is useless to ignore the fact that the success of mining enterprise must depend to a great extent upon the health and contentment of the labourers employed.

Diagrams.—These are of very great service in making a report intelligible. Those which may be recommended must vary with circumstances and with the form of the deposit. In the case of a vein, a plan, longitudinal section, and cross sections would fully illustrate its form; whilst a plan and several sections would be necessary in the case of an irregular deposit, or, perhaps, two or three plans at different horizons would be best. Sometimes a single diagram, either a plan or a section, would be of great service in explaining the allusions in a report.

The colouring may be such as to show either the richness of the various parts of the deposits, or the ground that has been worked during the period referred to by the report, compared with previous periods. Diagrams illustrating special matters were spoken of in the last section (p. 129).

Tabular Statements.—These ought to be set out in the simplest and clearest manner possible, and care should be taken that the headings to columns are self-explanatory; this is often not the case, because they are copied without thought from books in which, for brevity, the headings are curtailed.

As to the number of statements necessary there must, of course, be the essential profit and loss account and balance sheet; beyond these, from one to three other tables will, as a rule, be sufficient. If there are three, they might appropriately be: (1) Tabular statement of Ore Raised and Treated; (2) Analysis of Expenditure; (3) Statistical Summary. If one is thought sufficient, the third would be the best to adopt.

The following example of three tables for a gold mine may prove suggestive, though it must always be remembered that it is necessary to adopt forms suitable to the particular case in point, as those suitable for one mine may not be adapted for another. The examples of analyses given in Part III. will also be of some help here. It is scarcely necessary to remark that the weekly or monthly analyses should be of the same character as the yearly, so that the data collected for the one shall be available for the other.

---

* For methods, see relative chapters in Brough, *A Treatise on Mine-Surveying*, 6th edition, London, 1897; also Kirby, "The Sampling and Measurement of Ore Bodies," *Engineering and Mining Journal of New York*, vol. lix., 1895, pp. 196, 221, 241, and 247.

ORE RAISED AND TREATED.

Month.	Ore Raised.			Development.			Prospecting.	Battery.							Other Methods.			Extraction of Gold.		
	Quantity.								Bullion obtained.				Concentrated.							
	Gross (with moisture).	Net.	Gold Contents.	Shafts sunk.	Winzes risen or sunk.	Driving.	Boring or Sinking or Driving.	Ore Treated.	Total Quantity.	Per ton treated.	Fineness per 1000.	Gross Value.	Quantity.	Gold Contents.	Gold Contents of Tailings.	[Similar classification to "Battery," less the two columns for "Concentrates."]	Total Gold obtained.	Total Gross Value of Gold obtained.	Percentage of Gold contained in Ore which has been extracted.
Jan., Feb., &c.,			A																	B

Notes on above Table.—(A) This information, though of the very first importance, is oftentimes not determined with the care necessary to make it valuable. It can be obtained in two ways—either by sampling the ore before it goes through the mill and assaying the sample, or by sampling and assaying the tailings, and adding the amount of gold shown to the amount extracted from the ore. Great care is necessary in sampling; it is especially difficult to obtain a correct sample of tailings.

(B) This figure is very valuable, and ought to be always known and given in reports; but managers frequently omit it!

ANALYSIS OF EXPENDITURE.

	January.		February.		Totals.
	Total Amount.	Per Ton of Ore Raised.		Per Ton of Ore Raised.	Average per Ton of Ore Raised.
Raising Ore—					
Labour,					
Timber,					
Explosives,					
Stores,					
Machine Drills,					
Winding,					
Pumping, &c.,					
Total,					
Development,					
Prospecting,					
		Per Ton of Ore Treated.		Per Ton of Ore Treated.	Average per Ton Treated.
Extraction—					
Battery Labour,					
,, Stores,		A		A	A
,, Fuel,					
Other Methods,					
		Per Ton of Ore Raised.			
General Expenses—					
Salaries,					
Material, &c.,					
Machinery and Plant,					
Renewals and Repairs,					
Royalty and Rent,					
Rates and Taxes,					
Depreciation,					

MINE ACCOUNTS.

Notes on above Table.—(A) These costs to be useful for comparison must be worked out per ton of ore treated, as, for a particular month, the amount of ore *treated* might differ considerably from the amount of ore *raised*. (B) is got by dividing the total amount of cost for the month (B') by the tons of ore raised; and (C) is got by dividing the grand total (C') by the same amount.

It is evident that this table could be expanded or condensed to almost any extent, and so made to suit various circumstances. For instance, the total cost only of raising ore might be given; and, if thought sufficient, the costs for the year might alone be set out, and not for each month. On the other hand, the various costs could be analysed much more in detail by simply lengthening the table.

TABLE OF STATISTICS.

Year.	Capital.						Ore Raised.		Gold Extracted.		Per cent. of Total Gold in Ore which has been extracted.	Other cost per Ton of Ore	Total Cost		Value of Gold got.		Profit.	Dividends.
	Ordinary Shares.			Preference Shares.		Debentures.												
	No.	Value.	Amount.	No.	Value.	Amount.	Amount Net.	Cost per ton.	Amount.	Cost per ton of Ore.			Amount. Per ton of Ore.	Per oz. of Gold.	Amount. Per oz. of Gold.	Per ton of Ore.	Amount.	Per cent.
							tons.	s. d.	oz.	s. d.								

To multiply tables tends to confusion, and certainly makes it difficult to find the special information wished for. In the report of the Silver Mining Company, before referred to, there are no less than twelve statistical tables; but this by no means indicates either completeness of information or clearness of tabulating. Thus, there is no information as to the total metallic contents of the ore as it comes from the mine, and so there is no indication of the loss sustained in the various metallurgical operations; there is no analysis of costs; and it is only possible to get some idea as to the cost per ton of the various operations by an examination of the working account in connection with other tables, and by considerable calculation.

Information such as that contained in the above tables may often with advantage be plotted graphically, as described on p. 129.

The following example of a model balance sheet and Profit and Loss account is taken from the *Engineering and Mining Journal*, New York (vol. lxii., 1896, p. 170):—

(*Note.—The credits are printed below the debits instead of by their side as in the published balance-sheet.*)

ALASKA TREADWELL GOLD MINING COMPANY.—BALANCE-SHEET, MAY 31ST, 1896.

Dr.   CAPITAL AND LIABILITIES.

To capital stock —200,000 shares of $25 each,		$5,000,000.00
„ sundry creditors—		
Suspense cash account*—		
Douglas Island,	$21,775.97	
Current accounts—Douglas Island,	31,996.98	
„ —San Francisco,	25,802.50	
		79,575.45
„ surplus—Balance carried over from the year 1895,	$130,286.27	
„ profit and loss account, year ending May 31st, 1896,	497,342.22	
	$627,628.49	
Less dividends paid during year,	450,000.00	
Surplus carried over,		177,628.49
		$5,257,203.94

* Cash available for any exigency.

REPORTS OF MINING COMPANIES.

PROPERTY AND ASSETS.   Cr.

By mines, canals, and reduction works, ... $5,039,013.34
,, store supplies—
   Merchandise at Douglas Island, . . . $77,157.24
         ,,   in transit, . . .   10,025.69
                                        _____
                                         $87,182.93
   Wood on hand, . . .   11,382.00
   Coal on hand, . . .   2,459.59
   Extra mill machinery, . . .   8,254.32
   Potato account, . . .   116.13
   Rebate claims* in adjustment,   660.26
                                        _____
                                                                    110,055.23
,, cash at San Francisco, $80,188.50
   ,,   ,, Douglas Island, .   27,946.37
                                        _____
                                                                    108,134.87
                                                                  _____
                                                                  $5,257,203.94

Dr.   PROFIT AND LOSS ACCOUNT FOR YEAR ENDING 31ST MAY, 1896.

                                                   Per ton
                                                   of ore.
To operating costs—
   Mining 263,670 tons ore, ... $.5491 $144,787.68
   Milling 263,670 tons and concentrating 4,373$\frac{2}{10}$
      tons sulphurets, ...3476   91,671.34
   Chlorination of 4,397$\frac{1}{5}$ tons sulphurets, . . .1138   30,012.80
   General expenses, Douglas Island, ...0819   21,597.51
         ,,   San Francisco, ...0218   5,727.46
   London, office expense, ...0112   2,946.48
   Paris,   ,, ...0006   174.12
   Bullion charges, freight, insurance, &c., . .0372   9,807.12
   All construction charged directly to operating.

Total operating costs, ... $1.1632 $306,724.51
Net profit for year, ... 1.8862   497,342.22
                                         _____ _____
                                         $3.0494 $804,066.73

                                                                    Cr.
                                                   Per ton
                                                   of ore.
By bullion sold, ... $2.9689 $782,829.67
,, interest received. 0006   174.13
,, store profits, 12 months, ...0799   21,062.93
                                         _____ _____
                                         $3.0494 $804,066.73

It shows very plainly how various items contribute to the total cost per ton of ore, and how the profit resulted.

Directors' Report.—It is a question whether, in many cases, it would not be better to omit the Manager's Report altogether, and let the Directors' Report include all it is necessary to say about the mine and other matters, as the Directors can take a broader view of the effect of details on the whole, and can more readily free themselves from technicalities. If, however, the Manager's Report be printed, a part of the Directors' Report should be devoted

* Disputed claims.

to elucidating any obscure points in it and simplifying it, should that be in any degree necessary.

The Directors' Report should also contain, by way of commentary on the tabular statements, a simple explanation of the financial position of the Company; and finally, a general exposition of its present position and future prospects.

Mr. Pixley, upon this point, says : * " The majority of shareholders experience great difficulty in understanding Companies' accounts, even when they have been prepared with the object of affording full information, and the report of the Directors, which usually accompanies them, although it may refer to them, does not explain them ;" again, the Hon. C. J. Rhodes speaking, as chairman, at an ordinary general meeting of De Beers Consolidated Mines, Limited, said : † " In submitting to you the report of the Directors of the De Beers Consolidated Mines, together with the balance sheet for your approval, I would ask you to go through it with me in what I call an ordinary human way. We often read balance sheets and statements, and the average individual rises from the perusal of them no better informed than when he took his seat." Forthwith Mr. Rhodes proceeded to give a familiar and lucid explanation of the accounts in consideration, which fortunately has been preserved by appending it to the report. Would it not add greatly to the value of Companies' reports, in spite of some loss in elegance, if such familiar explanations were always embodied by the Directors? It is true that such explanations are not infrequently given verbally at meetings, as in the above instance, but, as a rule, they are not preserved, except in newspapers, and so no benefit from them accrues to the general body of shareholders.

Reports of Cost-Book Mines.—The report of a cost-book mine contains :—

1. A "Statement of Accounts," which is really a revenue account. On the debit side there are the various outgoings, chiefly labour costs and merchants' bills, the former being given in fortnightly totals, and the latter in monthly totals. On the credit side is the income, chiefly from sales of ore, each sale being given in detail.

2. List of ledger balances.

3. Analyses of labour cost and merchants' bills.

4. Average weekly sales of ore, and perhaps average price, compared with the last period.

5. Agents' report, which is chiefly an account of the condition of the mine, or rather notes on the different points of interest with a few general remarks. Throughout, the reader's personal acquaintance with the mine is assumed.

6. The resolutions passed at the meeting, (for these reports are always printed and distributed *after* each meeting).

There may, or there may not be a short Report of the Committee referring to financial matters. Occasionally a list of the adventurers is sent out with the report, and still more rarely an account of the meetings is appended.

The absence of a balance sheet has already been mentioned (pp. 91 and 114).

The following are examples of 1 and 2, in the above list, from a well-known Cornish mine :—‡

(*Note.*—*The credits are printed below the debits instead of by their side as in the actual statement.*)

---

* Pixley, *The Shareholder's Handbook*, London, 1884, p. 17.
† Sixth Annual Report of the De Beers Consolidated Mines, Limited, 1894, p. 25.
‡ An example is also given in *The Accountants' Students' Journal*, vol. iii., 1885-1886, pp. 49, 65, 98.

REPORTS OF MINING COMPANIES. 135

..........................MINES.

Dr.   STATEMENT OF ACCOUNTS, MAY 16TH, 1893.

				£	s.	d.	£	s.	d.
To Labour Cost paid	January 21st, 1893,			1,499	12	7			
,, ,,	February 4th, 1893,			1,408	12	11			
,, ,,	February 18th, 1893,			1,551	0	5			
,, ,,	March 4th, 1893,			1,379	5	0			
,, ,,	March 18th, 1893,			1,564	5	8			
,, ,,	April 1st, 1893,			1,366	10	0			
,, ,,	April 15th, 1893,			1,637	17	1			
,, ,,	April 29th, 1893,			1,367	4	1			
							11,774	7	9
,, January Merchants' Bills,		1,118	3	7					
Coal,		611	19	7					
					1,730	3	2		
,, February Merchants' Bills,		959	16	1					
Coal,		601	13	3					
					1,561	9	4		
,, March Merchants' Bills,		865	14	7					
Coal,		617	18	5					
					1,483	13	0		
,, April Merchants' Bills,		758	12	3					
Coal,		534	12	1					
					1,293	4	4		
							6,068	9	10
,, Doctors' Pence,							144	3	6
,, Tehidy Estates, Dues,							458	16	6
,, West Cornwall Hospital,							26	5	0
,, Royal Cornwall Infirmary,							2	2	0
,, Camborne District Nurse Fund,							3	3	0
,, Vice Warden's Assessment,							20	6	9
,, The National Boiler and General Insurance Co.,							2	2	3
,, Cornish Bank, Limited, Interest and Cheques,							38	15	0
,, Income Tax, on Account,							175	0	0
,, Employers' Liability Assurance Co., Limited, on Account,							75	0	0
							18,788	11	7
	Divisible Balance,						2,829	0	2
							21,617	11	9

By Sales of Tin Ore, viz.— *Cr.*

1893.		T.	C.	Q.	LBS.				£	s.	d.	£	s.	d.
Jan. 18.	Redruth Tin Co.,	6	6	2	9	at £50	7	6	318	16	5			
,, 18.	Williams, Harvey, & Co.,	6	1	3	0	at 49	15	0	302	17	0			
,, 18.	Williams, Harvey, & Co.,	4	0	0	0	at 50	7	6	201	10	0			
,, 18.	Consolidated Tin Co., Ltd.,	7	3	2	3	at 50	7	6	361	10	0			
Feb. 1.	Cornish Tin Co.,	36	5	1	9	at 51	2	6	1854	2	7			
,, 1.	Cornish Tin Co.,	8	16	0	17	at 51	5	0	451	7	9			
	&c., &c.,	&c.,	&c.,						&c.					
May 10.	Consolidated Tin Co., Ltd.,	8	13	3	7	at 47	12	6	413	17	9			
												20,894	19	5
		413	13	2	0									

1893.	Slime Tin Sold.													
Feb. 1.	Cornish Tin Co.,	2	0	0	2	at £31	10	0	63	0	7			
	&c., &c.,	&c.,	&c.,						&c.					
May 10.	Consolidated Tin Co., Ltd.,	2	1	1	12	at 25	5	0	52	4	3			
												461	8	9
		16	2	1	1									
	Illogan Parish,											0	18	9
	Extra Carriage,											21	11	5
	Employers' Liability Assurance Co., Limited,											99	14	8
	Discount off Merchants' Bills,											138	18	9
												21,617	11	9

136   MINE ACCOUNTS.

Dr.
1893.
May 12. To Paid on Account of Machinery for ...., . £1,500 0 0
         ,, Adventurers' Balance, ... 4,384 12 3
                                                            ─────────────
                                                            £5,884 12 3

                                                                Cr.
1893.
May 12. Divisible Balance brought down, ... £2,829 0 2
         Balance from last Account, January 24th, 1893,   . 3,055 12 1
                                                            ─────────────
                                                            £5,884 12 3

Dr.
1893.
May 16. To Dividend of 7s. 6d. per each 6,000th Share declared this day, . £2,250 0 0
  ,, 16. ,, Balance carried to the next account, ... 2,134 12 3
                                                            ─────────────
                                                            £4,384 12 3

                                                                Cr.
1893.
May 12. By Balance brought down,   . £4,384 12 3
                                                            ─────────────
                                                            £4,384 12 3

Dr.   LEDGER BALANCES, MAY 12TH, 1893.
To Adventurers' Balance, ... £4,384 12 3
,, Income Tax, ...   175 0 0
,, Employers' Liability Co., Limited, ...   75 0 0
                                                            ─────────────
                                                            £4,634 12 3

                                                                Cr.
By Cornish Bank, Limited, Cash, ... £550 15 6
  ,,   ,,   ,,   Bills Receivable, .   . 3,943 10 5
                                                  ───────── £4,494 5 11
,, Club Account, ...   140 6 4
                                                            ─────────────
                                                            £4,634 12 3

CHAPTER XV.—STATISTICS.

UNDER this head we shall briefly consider the information which is collected and published with the view of exhibiting the condition of the mining industry of a country. Such publication may be looked upon as a national mining report; just as a Company requires a report at the year's end of the work of the year, and a balancing of its financial position, in order to see exactly how matters stand, and have data for directing its future course, so a country requires a report of its mining industry, in order to estimate the importance of the industry, judge of its growth or decline, encourage its development, husband its resources, and legislate for its benefit and safety. Statistics, when sufficiently full, are also of value to individuals, and are further of international importance.

In the reports of mining companies, suitable tabular statements are of great value, but they do not suffice without explanatory matter; in like manner statistical tables require interpretation from an expert for their full appreciation. Diagrams are of very great value in connection with statistics, inasmuch as the relative importance of quantities is often more quickly and accurately estimated by the eye when they are plotted as a diagram, than can be done from figures; further, the impression upon the brain produced by a diagram is more readily retained.

In England, previous to 1845, there was no attempt to collect mineral and mining statistics systematically. Some information had, however, been given in reports* of Special Committees and Commissioners, and Custom House returns of the imports and exports of minerals had been issued since the early part of the present century. Private individuals had also published statistical tables, which, though fragmentary, are still of interest—particular mention may be made of Pryce,† Lemon, and Carne.‡ Sir Charles Lemon, especially, published a valuable paper §; the data he gives conform closely to our present idea of what mining statistics should contain, in that he does not confine himself simply to quantities and value of ore raised, but gives figures relating to the number of persons employed, wages earned, and health of miners.

The Mining Record Office was established as a branch of the Geological Survey in 1840, on a recommendation by a Committee of the British Association for the Advancement of Science. Its primary object, however, was to collect and preserve plans of abandoned mines. It was not until Mr. Robert Hunt was appointed Keeper in 1845 that any attempt was made to collect statistics. As the first result of his labours in this direction, Mr. Hunt published in 1847, "A Notice of the Copper and Tin raised in Cornwall,"‖ chiefly historical; and in the following year he published " Statistics of Lead and Copper." giving quantities only, for the years 1845, 1846, 1847.¶ This was followed in 1853 by "Statistics of the Produce of Copper, Tin, Lead, and Silver from the Mines of the United Kingdom, with the Imports and Exports of these metals from 1848 to 1852;"** also a "Note on Coal Raised and Iron Made at present (December, 1852) in South Staffordshire";†† and in 1855 the first annual volume of Mineral Statistics was published as a memoir of the Geological Survey. It recorded the quantities and values of copper, lead, tin, and silver ores produced, imported, and exported for the years 1853 and 1854; and for 1854 statistics of coal and iron, the number of persons employed in mining operations, and a list of collieries. A volume of this character was henceforward published every year from the Mining Record Office until 1882, statistics of other minerals being gradually added; but the information as to the number of persons employed about mines was never repeated. The information supplied to the Mining Record Office was always voluntary.

In the meantime, statistics relating to coal and accidents in coal mines were being published by the Inspectors of Mines in their annual reports.‡‡ The first Act providing for the inspection of coal mines was passed in 1850; and

* See footnote to p. 140.
† Pryce, William, *Mineralogia Cornubiensis*, London, 1778, p. xv.
‡ Carne, Joseph, "Statistics of the Tin Mines in Cornwall." *Journal of the Statistical Society of London*, vol. ii., 1839, p. 261.
§ Lemon, Sir Charles, " The Statistics of the Copper Mines of Cornwall." *Journal of the Statistical Society of London*, vol. i., 1838, p. 65.
‖ *Memoirs of the Geological Survey*, 1847, London, vol. i.
¶ *Memoirs of the Geological Survey*, 1848, London, vol. ii., part 2, pp. 703-717.
** *Records of the School of Mines*, 1853, London, vol. i., part 4.
†† *Records of the School of Mines*, 1853, London, vol. i., part 2.
‡‡ See introduction to *Mineral Statistics for 1882* for fuller information.

138   MINE ACCOUNTS.

the first Inspectors' report was published in 1851. This contained statistics of the coal produced in several districts during 1850; and in succeeding reports figures from other districts were included. In 1864 a tabular statement of the quantity of coal wrought, number of persons employed, and ratios of accidents in the different districts, was commenced. At this time, as in the case of the Mining Record Office, information relating to the production of coal and persons employed was supplied voluntarily to the Inspectors, though notices of accidents were compulsory; returns of the imports and exports were supplied by the Customs House authorities. In 1872 the Coal Mines Regulation Act, and Metalliferous Mines Regulation Act were passed, and these provided that annual returns of minerals worked and persons employed at mines, should be made to the Inspectors; and from this time onward, their statistics were founded on these returns.

Thus there were two sets of statistics, one published from the Mining Record Office, and based upon voluntary information, the other issued by the Home Office and, after 1872, based upon information compulsorily supplied to the Inspectors; this state of things was evidently undesirable, consequently the Mining Record Office was transferred to the Home Office in 1883, since which date only one set of mining and mineral statistics has been issued.

The volume of *Mineral Statistics for 1882*, published in 1883, recorded the quantities and values of minerals worked in the United Kingdom, also imports and exports of minerals and metals, and, in addition, it contained tables showing the quantities of mineral produced, &c., in other countries, extracted from the *Statistique de l'Industrie Minérale en France et en Algérie*. The volume for 1883 contained (besides statistics of the production, importation, and exportation of minerals and metals) an account of persons employed, of accidents, and of the ratio of accidents and deaths to the number of persons employed for each inspection district in the following form:—

District.	Persons Employed in and about Mines.	Tons of Mineral Wrought.	Separate Fatal Accidents.	Lives Lost by Accidents.	Persons Employed.		Tons of Mineral Wrought.		No. of Mines.
					Per Fatal Accident.	Per Life Lost.	Per Fatal Accident.	Per Life Lost.	

An account of the mineral products of our Colonies was also added, which has found a place in each report since published. In the report for 1887, diagrams showing the fluctuations in the prices of metals were first introduced, and have been given regularly since that year. In 1888 the number of people employed and statistics of accidents ceased to appear in *Mineral Statistics*, but continued to be issued in *Summaries of Statistics of Mines and Minerals*, as heretofore.

Of late years there have been published separately from the Home Office * :—

1. Summaries of Statistics.
2. Separate report by each inspector for his own district.
3. The Mineral Statistics of the United Kingdom.
4. List of Mines at work.   } Formerly appended to *Mineral Statistics*.
5. List of Plans of abandoned Mines.

The report of each inspector (2) contains details concerning persons employed, mineral output, accidents, and any prosecutions for offences, together with general observations on the condition of the district.

* See *Report of the Departmental Committee on Mining and Mineral Statistics*, 1895. p. 1, *et seq*.

The *Mineral Statistics* (3) contains—

(*a*) Particulars of the output and value of minerals, and the quantity and value of metals contained in the various ores.

(*b*) Statistics relating to the imports and exports of minerals and metals, railway and canal traffic of coal, salt, &c.; shipments of coal, clay, and other minerals coastwise; particulars of blast furnaces, giving the production of pig iron and the quantity of iron ore and coal used in its manufacture; the average weekly prices of coal and metals in the London market; lists of smelters of ores, with their addresses; also an appendix giving the output and value of all the minerals raised in the British Colonies and Possessions. The book also contains maps showing the Mines Inspection districts, and a list of the names and addresses of the Inspectors.

In 1884 Professor Le Neve Foster * pointed out that the method of working out ratios of accidents to the total number of persons employed about mines led to misleading results, as it showed the occupation of the ore miner to be less hazardous than that of the collier, whereas, if underground workers alone are considered, the risk is about equal in the two cases.

The Royal Commission on Mining Royalties, appointed in 1889, thought the mineral statistics could be improved, and suggested that accurate information should be collected and published, relating to the following amongst other matters†:—

1. The quantities of coal used for manufacturing and domestic purposes respectively.
2. The amounts of royalties and wayleaves.
3. The average price of coal at the pit's mouth, and at various points of consumption.
4. The wages and hours of labour of miners.
5. Imports and exports of mineral.
6. The comparison of the progress of the mining industry in the United Kingdom and in foreign countries.

To this, they added, "Where necessary, additional statutory powers should be conferred on the department,‡ to enable it to collect the necessary information, due care being taken to prevent the disclosure of individual returns."

A Departmental Committee, of which Professor Le Neve Foster was chairman, was appointed in 1893 to consider the whole question of Mining and Mineral Statistics, in view of the suggestions of the Royal Commission on Mining Royalties.

Early in 1895 they issued a valuable report discussing the recommendations of the Royal Commission, and suggesting the best manner of their adoption. They further suggested that the following separate publications (compare with list on p. 138) should be issued each year in the order given :—

1. Early Return of Fatal Accidents.
2. Summaries of Statistics relating to Mines and Minerals.
3. List of Plans of Abandoned Mines.
4. List of Mines and Quarries at Work.
5. Separate Reports of the Inspectors of Mines.
6. Mineral Statistics of the United Kingdom.
7. General Report on the Mining Industry of the United Kingdom.

They further recommend that (*a*) in all these publications, uniformity in arranging the information should be carefully maintained. (*b*) In the "*Summaries*" (2 of above list) the death-rate should be calculated per 1,000

* *Report of British Association for the Advancement of Science for* 1884, p. 868.
† *Final Report of the Royal Commission on Mining Royalties*, 1893, p. 13.
‡ *i.e.*, Of Mines.

persons employed, and per 1,000,000 tons of mineral raised; and also be calculated separately for underground men; in the "*Mineral Statistics*" (6) the produce of each mine should be given. This had been done hitherto for Metalliferous Mines, but not for Collieries.

These recommendations have been adopted as far as was possible without additional statutory power; for, as this has not yet been granted, the Inspectors of Mines have no authority to ask for information relative to royalties and wayleaves, or hours of labour and wages of workpeople. The seven publications have (1895), however, been issued in the order suggested; and, in addition to other improvements in the Statistics, the *First Annual General Report upon the Mineral Industry of the United Kingdom for 1894* was issued in 1895, followed by the *Second* of this new series last year.

The first report is prefaced by a brief outline of the laws which regulate the mineral workings of the United Kingdom. Part I. contains an account of the workpeople employed in or about mines. Part II. treats of minerals raised, coloured diagrams being used to bring out the more important facts. Part III. relates to accidents, which are classified in various ways. In Part IV. prosecutions are tabulated. Part V. relates to general matters, such as notes on the separate reports of the Inspectors. The last Part—VI.—is the most considerable in the book. It gives an account of the mining industry in each country of the world, the countries being dealt with in alphabetical order. The appendices include a glossary of terms used in the Inspectors' reports, which may not be familiar to the general reader.

Various statistics relating to mines and minerals have been published from time to time in reports* of Commissions and Special Committees; and in the form of Returns. Particular mention may be made of the *Report of the Commissioners appointed to inquire into the Condition of Mines to which the Act 23 and 24 Vic. chap.* 151 *does not apply*, 1864; and the *Report of the Commissioners appointed to inquire into several matters relating to Coal*, 1871. The former contains much valuable information relating to the health and safety of persons employed in metalliferous mining, and the latter, *inter alia*, valuable statistics relating to the production and consumption of coal.

The Board of Trade frequently publishes information and statistics relative to mines and minerals in its monthly journals—*Labour Gazette, Board of Trade Journal*, and *Trade and Navigation*; also in its *Annual Statistical Abstract*, and other occasional pamphlets. The Foreign Office Consular Reports also often contain information relative to the mining industry in other countries; and lastly, the *Annual Statement of Trade*, published by the Board of Customs, has figures relating to minerals.

* The following list, though probably incomplete, may be of service:—
  Report of Committee on the State of Copper Mines and Copper Trade, 1799.
  Reports of Committees on the Coal Trade, 1830 and 1838.
  Reports of Select Committees on Coal Mines, 1852, 1853, 1866.
  Reports of Commission on several matters relating to Coal, 1871.
  Report of Select Committee on Coal, 1873.
  Accidents:—
  Reports of Committees on Accidents in Coal Mines, 1835, 1843, 1847, 1849, 1852, 1854, 1867.
  Relating chiefly to Work-people:—
  Report of Children's Employment Commission, 1842.
  Reports of Commissioner to inquire into State of Mining Population, &c., 1844 to 1859.
  Report of Commissioners on Condition of Mines to which the Act 23 and 24 Vic. chap. 151 *does not apply*, 1864. (Chairman, Lord Kinnaird.)
  Return of Hours of Labour of Persons employed in and about Mines, 1890.
  Return of Rates of Wages in Mines and Quarries, 1891.

The summaries and analyses made at each mine should be so arranged that they can be used for filling up the annual returns to be sent to the Inspector of Mines. This saves labour, and further makes it possible to forward the returns with the least delay. Statistics lose something of their value if they are very late in publication. Official forms for returns are prescribed.*

Yearly volumes of mining statistics, or annual mining reports containing statistics, are published by almost all civilised countries.

In France an excellent volume of statistics is published annually bearing the title *Statistique de l'Industrie Minérale et des Appareils à vapeur en France et en Algérie*. The main divisions are as follow:—

MINING CONCESSIONS.
MINES.
   Combustible Minerals—
      Production, number of workers, wages, imports and exports, value, consumption
   Iron Ores—
      Production, number of workers, wages, imports and exports, consumption.
   Other metalliferous substances.
   Bitumen and other substances.
   General *résumé.*
   Persons working at mines.
   Financial results.
QUARRIES.
   Statistics of accidents.
   Mineral waters.
   State of the Mineral Industry in the Colonies.
METALLURGICAL WORKS—
   Iron.
   Metals other than iron.
   Asphalts, &c.
STEAM ENGINES—
   Steam engines on *terra firma* other than locomotives.
   Locomotives.
   Steam engines on boats.
   Accidents.
INTERNATIONAL STATISTICS.
   Comparative table of mineral products of the principal countries.
       ,,   metallurgical products.
       ,,   precious metals.

Numerous diagrams showing production, consumption, and price of different minerals and metals in France, for many years past, are given.

It will be observed that the financial results of working mines are included, and also statistics relating to steam engines.

In the United States, the separate mining States have their own reports, and there is also a yearly volume, prepared by the Geological Survey, entitled *The Mineral Resources of the United States*. Ohio, for instance, publishes annually a *Mine Inspector's Report*, in which are given statistics relating to—
                Production of Minerals,
                Persons Employed,
                Accidents,

whilst in California, the Mining Report is the *Bi-Annual Report of the State Mineralogist*. It gives the production of gold and silver in dollars, and of

* Much fuller forms are recommended in the *Report of the Departmental Committee on Mining and Mineral Statistics*, 1895, pp. 26 to 30, which would no doubt come into use were statutory powers to that effect obtained.

other metals in tons; and it contains much information about the geology, ore deposits, and mines of the State. Detailed mineral statistics are given in the annual " Bulletin."

In *The Mineral Resources of the United States*, the metals or minerals are taken separately ; the production is given and compared with that of other countries ; and any points of interest, such as new deposits found during the year, or technical developments, are discussed.

In Australia separate reports are published by each of the Colonies. Some of these are very full and valuable. Especial mention may be made of those issued by Victoria and New South Wales.

The first official mining report of the South African Republic (for 1894) was issued in 1895. It contains reports by the Inspectors on points of interest and tabulated information chiefly relating to—

> Claims.
> Expenditure at Mines and Price of Stores.
> Machinery, Engines, and Boilers.
> Ore Raised, Persons Employed, Gold obtained.
> Quantity and value of Coal raised.
> Wages arranged according to trades.
> Accidents.

The report is very complete and contains much information not usually given in annual mining reports.

In Cape Colony a yearly pamphlet, entitled *Reports of the Inspector of Mines, Kimberley, and Inspector of Claims, Barkly West*, is published. The former report contains the number of persons employed, accidents, and general information relating to the diamond mines of Kimberley. The annual *Statistical Register of the Colony of the Cape of Good Hope* gives the weight and value of the diamonds obtained, number of persons employed, and accidents at the diamond mines; and, in addition, the production of copper ore, coal, salt, and gold in the Colony.

Private enterprise, although not supported by legal enactments, has done valuable service in collecting mining statistics. For many years the *Engineering and Mining Journal of New York* (Editor, R. P. Rothwell), has published accurate statistics of the mineral productions of the United States much earlier than they have been issued from official sources; and since 1893 there has been issued from the office of that periodical an annual volume entitled, *The Mineral Industry ; Its Statistics, Technology, and Trade in the United States and Other Countries*. This is a publication valued by all who are interested in mining. It contains under the head of each metal or mineral, an account of the mode of occurrence, especially mentioning any newly discovered deposits; methods of working, if there is anything of note to describe ; recent improvements in treatment or metallurgy ; and statistics showing the production of each country. Further, under the name of each country it gives an account of the mineral industry in that country. This is followed by a short account of the stock market for the year and, finally, there are special articles on matters of interest and importance to the mining community.

The Witwatersrand Chamber of Mines publishes monthly a tabular return of the production of gold at the greater number of mines on the Rand, showing, for each mine, the quantity of ore treated, yield and value of gold, for each process of extraction used. An annual report is also published by the Chamber. The Association of Mines of the South African Republic likewise publishes an annual report. It contains statistics relating to mines not included in the report of the Rand Chamber of Mines.

Looking at the publication of mining statistics generally, it is to be regretted that there is so great a lack of uniformity, both in the matter given, and in the manner of giving it, as to make comparisons difficult or impossible.

The mining population is often neglected; in some reports, no statistics relative to workmen are given, though the majority state the number of persons employed about mines and of accidents; but in no case, it would appear, are vital statistics * showing the relative healthiness or unhealthiness of the industry systematically collected and published.

In 1893 Professor Le Neve Foster read a paper † before the International Mining Congress held at Chicago, pointing out some of the ways in which the mining statistics of various countries differ, and making various suggestions. The following brief summary of some of the points mentioned and suggestions made will be of interest:—

Production of Minerals and Metals.—1. The standards of weight employed are very various. It was suggested that, in addition to local weights, metric equivalents be given.

2. Some countries include in their statistics substances omitted by others. An international agreement by mining engineers as to the definition of the term "mineral" would be an advantage.

3. It was suggested that there should always be one general table showing the production of all the minerals worked in a country. This is sometimes omitted, which causes labour in searching through a report, besides the possibility of some omission, if a general view of the mineral production of a country is wanted.

4. Some countries give the production of mineral before it is dressed—that is, of raw mineral; others, of dressed mineral. It was suggested that the weight of dressed ore, or mineral, or rock, would be the more valuable quantity to record.

Value of Minerals Produced.—This should not include freight.

Persons employed in and about Mines.—Those working underground should always be distinguished from those employed above ground, and so should males from females. The number of persons employed is one of the best gauges of the importance of a mine, or of the entire industry in a State.

Death-Rate from Accidents.—This might conveniently be calculated per 1,000, and should be calculated separately for underground workers and surface hands.

Vital Statistics.—These should be collected, as they are of very great importance in connection with legislation to promote the health and prosperity of miners; hence, indirectly, they have an important bearing on the mining industry, and so on the welfare of the State.

Finally, it was suggested that each country should prepare a few general tables, which could be collated by some central body and published as *The Mineral Statistics of the World*, with references to the official publications containing details.

* Death-rates for the mining industry in this country were worked out by Dr. Ogle, and published in the *Supplement to the Forty-fifth Annual Report of the Registrar of Births, Deaths, and Marriages in England*, London, 1885, p. 25, *et seq.* There are also some vital statistics given in the *Report of the Commission appointed to inquire into the condition of Mines* to which the Act 23 and 24 *Vic.*, ch. 151, does not apply, pp. 10, 29, and 35; also Appendix B, p. 154, *et seq.*

† "Mining and Mineral Statistics," *Transactions of the American Institute of Mining Engineers*, vol. xxii., 1894, p. 95.

BIBLIOGRAPHY.

Although many of the writings and lectures mentioned below have already been referred to, yet the following list may prove convenient:—

I. BOOKS RELATING WHOLLY TO MINE ACCOUNTS AND ALLIED MATTERS.

Gottschalk, C. G. Die Grundlagen des Rechnungswesens und ihre Anwendung auf industrielle Anstalten, insbesondere auf Bergbau, Hütten- und Fabrik-Betrieb. Leipzig, 1865, pp. 467.
Mannlicher, G. Leitfaden der Verrechnungskunde von Montanwerken nach dem Systeme der doppelten kaufmännischen Buchhaltung. Graz, 1865.
Löhe, W. Die Materialen-Verwaltung für Fabriken, Berg- und Hütten-Werke. Elberfeld, 1879.
Lange, C. F. R. Das Grubenhaushalts-, Kassen- und Rechnungswesen. Freiberg in Sachsen, 1885, pp. 243.
Oriol. Contabilidad Minera. Madrid, 1894, pp. 87.
Brown, N. Gold Mining Accounts. Glasgow, 1897.

II. BOOKS WITH A SECTION ON MINE ACCOUNTS.

Leo, W. *Neuer Schauplatz der Bergwerke*, vol. xiii. "Grubenhaushalt." Quedlinburg und Leipzig, 1845-48.
Andre, G. G. Coal Mining, vol. ii. London, 1876, p. 521.
Baker, W. C. M. System of Accounts. Columbus, Ohio, 1876, p. 123.
Burat, A. Cours d'Exploitation des Mines. 2nd Ed. Paris, 1876, pp. 620 to 633.
Callon, J. Lectures on Mining, vol. iii., 1886, pp. 184-186.
Linkenbach, C. Die Aufbereitung der Erze. Berlin, 1887, pp. 148-150.
Hatch and Chalmers. Gold Mines of the Rand. London, 1895, pp. 259-263, and 266-270.
Bulman and Redmayne. Colliery Working and Management. London, 1896, pp. 64-107.

III. LECTURES, PAPERS, AND ARTICLES.

"Cost-Book Companies." *Accountants' Students' Journal.* London, vol. iii., 1885-86, pp. 49, 65, 98.
Attlee, T. M. E. "Colliery Accounts" (lecture). *Accountant*, vol. xi., London, 1885, pp. 576-579.
Evans. R. J. "Colliery Accounts" (lecture). *Accountant*, vol. xii., 1886, p. 51.
Van de Linde, Gérard. "Collieries" (lecture). *Accountant*, vol. xiv., 1888, pp. 287, 301, 319.
Greig, James. "Colliery Auditing" (lecture). *Accountant*, vol. xvi., 1891, p. 201.
Ludlow, Edwin. "The Subdivision of Mining Accounts." *Engineering and Mining Journal*, vol. lii. New York, 1891, p. 506.
Carey. "Colliery Cost Sheets." *Trans. National Association of Colliery Managers*, vol. v. London, 1893, p. 99.
"Colliery Accounts." *Accountant*, vol. xix., 1893, pp. 796, 811, 832, 852.
James. "Collieries: their Management and Accounts." *Trans. Chartered Accountants' Students' Society of London* for 1894, p. 134.
Salisbury. "Mining Accounts." *Trans. Incorporated Accountants' Students' Society of London* for 1894, p. 69.
Prest. "Colliery Cost Sheets." *Trans. Federated Institute of Mining Engineers*, vol. viii., 1894-95, p. 326; and vol. ix., 1894-95, p. 239.

INDEX.

A

ACCIDENT clubs, 22.
Accounts, chief ledger, 79, 96.
 Bad debts, 83.
 Bills, 84, 93.
 Cash, 83, 93, 97.
 Classification, 81, 82.
 Discount and Interest, 85.
 Ledger, 79, 80.
 Nominal, 80, 96.
 Personal, 80, 83, 99.
 Product, 85.
 Profit and Loss, 86, 90, 95. 101. 128, 133.
 Real, 80, 81.
 Revenue, see *Profit and Loss*.
 Stores, 83.
 Wages, 83, 99.
 Working, 86, 100.
Accounts sent to Head Office, 76.
Advantages of accounts, 1.
Agreements with workmen, 4.
Alaska-Treadwell Gold Mining Company, 132.
Allotment book, 119.
American Journals, 88.
Analyses—
 Cost, 67, 131.
 Labour, 66.
 Mineral, 57, 131.
 Stores, 69, 71.
 Wages, 68, 70.
Assay book, 53, 126.
Association of Mines, South African Republic, 142.
Attlee, T.M.E., 106, 109, 144.
Australia, 20, 142.
Authority to fire shots, 125.
Average wages book, 27.

B

BALANCE sheet, 90, 101, 113, 132.
Balancing stores, 44, 98.
"Bargain" work, 14.
Barruelo colliery, 62, 74.
Benefit Clubs, 22.
Blacksmiths' book, 25.
Bills, 80, 84.
Bill books, 79, 85, 93.
Bonuses, 20, 106.
Boring, Record of, 126.
British Statistics, 137.

C

CALIFORNIA, 141.
Carne, 137.

Cash book, 79, 83, 93.
Chamber of Mines, Rand, 142.
Check-weigher, 16.
Chili, 103.
Coal book, Cornish, 45.
 ,, Journal, 52.
 ,, Mines Regulation Act, 1887, 10, 16, 122, 124, 138.
 ,, Mines Regulation Act, 1896, 122.
 ,, raised, daily return, 61, 62.
 ,, ,, summary, 61, 62.
 ,, sales, 46, 49.
 ,, supplied to workmen, 24.
 ,, ticket, 24.
 ,, washed, return, 62.
Colliers, see *Workmen*.
Colorado, 11, 14, 21, 23, 27, 77.
Companies Act, 1862, 86, 90, 116, 118, 120, 127.
 ,, working mines, 111.
Consignment book, Coal, 50.
Continent, 14.
Contract book, Rand, 19.
 ,, work, 14.
Contracts for sales, 46.
 ,, supply of stores, 37, 38.
Conveying mineral, Payment for, 17.
Copper ore sales, 48.
Cornwall, 11, 14, 17, 18, 21, 22, 23, 25, 26, 30, 42, 45, 47, 49, 113, 116, 134, 137.
Cost book Companies, 91, 113, 134.
Costs, Analyses of, 67, 131.
"Creditor," 79.
Cumberland, 25, 63, 103.
Cyanide treatment return, 60.

D

DAY-BOOK, 88.
 ,, Coal, 52.
Day-work book, 12, 30.
Dead-work, 14.
De Beers Company, 9, 17, 18, 19, 23, 41, 42, 57, 68, 129, 134.
Debentures, 118.
"Debtor," 79.
Declaration, Railway, 51.
Deductions, 4, 16, 22.
Depreciation, 109.
Diagrams of costs, &c., 76, 130, 132.
 ,, of redemption of capital, 104.
 ,, in reports, 130.
Diamond mines, see *De Beers Co.*
Directors' reports, 133.
Dividends, 106.
Double entry, 79.
Driving, Payment for, 14.
Due-bills, 30.

10

INDEX.

E

ENGAGEMENT of workmen, 4.
Engineering and Mining Journal, 75, 130, 132, 142, 144.
Evans, R. J., 52, 106.
Exploitation, Payment for, 15.

F

FACTORY and Workshop Acts, 10, 14, 126.
Ferreira mine, 60.
Foreign mines—
   Agreement for service in, 7.
   Sending accounts home, 76.
Foster, C. Le Neve, 17, 21, 22, 139, 143.
Foxdale mine, 11, 34, 46.
French statistics, 141.
Furness, 23, 25, 27, 28, 43, 103.

G

GALLOWAY, W., 18, 31.
Glen Lead Mining Co., 91.
Gold ore sales, 55.
Graphic analyses of cost, &c., 76, 104, 130, 132.

H

HARTZ, 17.
Hodbarrow mine, 25.
Hoskold, H. D., 48, 104, 107, 109.

I

INSPECTIONS, Reports of, 122.
Inventory, 90.
Invoices, 38, 51, 53.
Iron ore sales, 46.
Isle of Man, see *Foxdale mine*.

J

JOURNAL, 79, 87, 94.
  ,, Coal, 52.

K

KAFFIRS, 10, 13.
Kimberley, see *De Beers Co.*

L

LABOUR analyses, 66.
Lancashire, 5, 25, 50, see also *Furness*.
Land-sales, 50, 51.
Lead ore sales, 47.
Ledger, 79, 96.
  ,, Stores, 44.
  ,, Tutwork, 30.
Leicestershire, 25.

Lemon, Sir C., 137.
Limited Liability Companies, 116.
Linkenbach, C., 64.
Llanbradach colliery, 18, 27, 28, 31, 32, 41, 44, 62, 71.

M

MANAGERS' reports, 129.
Mansfeld, 103.
Materials, see *Stores*.
Measuring book, 15.
Metalliferous Mines Reg. Act, 1872, 10, 17, 122, 126.
Mine Cost and Value Book, 74.
Mineral Industry, 142.
  ,, of U.K., 140.
Mineral raised, &c., summaries, 57, 131.
Mineral Resources of U.S., 142.
Miners, see *Workmen*.
Mining Journal, 116.
Mining Record Office, 137.
Missouri, 47.
Munro, 20.

N

NATIVES, S. Africa, 10, 12.
New South Wales, 20.
North Wales, 21.
Notices to Inspectors, 14, 123, 124, 126.
  ,, under Truck Act, 1896, 4.

O

OHIO, 141.
Order book, 40, 50.
Orders, 38, 50.
Ore raised and treated, 60, 61, 63, 65, 131.
Oriel, 10, 62, 63, 74, 76, 88.
Overtime, 13.

P

PAY-SHEETS, 26, 28, 29.
Pay-tickets, 33.
Paying men, 33.
Payment for driving, 14.
  ,, ,, exploitation, 15.
  ,, ,, manual transport, 17.
  ,, ,, sinking, 14.
"Pays," Periods between, 11.
Permits to fire shots, 125.
Piece work, 14.
"Posting," 79, 80.
Premiums and Bonuses, 20.
Private partnerships, 112.
Profit and Loss, 2 (see also *Accounts*).
Pryce, W., 137.

Q

QUENAST, 21.
Quotations for stores, 36.

INDEX. 147

R

RAND, 8, 11, 12, 19, 23, 25, 27, 28, 55, 60, 72, 103, 109, 142.
Reasons for Accounts, 1.
Redemption of Capital, 102.
Register, accidents, 127.
„ holidays, 14.
„ overtime, 14.
„ share, 79, 82, 115, 118.
„ young persons, &c., 10.
Rent book, 23, 24.
Reports of Inspections, 122.
„ Yearly, &c., 127.
Requisition book, 36
Reserve fund, 110.
Returns, Annual statistical, 137, 139, 141.
Rio Tinto, 17, 27, 28, 103.

S

SAFETY of Workmen, 3.
Sales, 46.
Sampling book, 22.
Share certificate book, 120.
„ ledger or register, 79, 82, 115, 118.
Shares, 117.
Sick clubs, 22.
„ pay book, 23.
Silver ore sales, 47, 53.
Sinking, Payment for, 14.
Sliding scales, 7, 20.
South Africa, 14, 142 (see also *De Beers Co.* and *Rand*).
South Wales, 17 (see also *Llanbradach*).
Spain, 10, 11, 62, 74 (see also *Rio Tinto*).
Stannaries Act, 1887, 11, 17, 113, 115.
Stannaries Act, 1896, 113.
Statistical returns, Annual, 137.
Statistics, Mining, 3, 136.
Stocks, 117.
Stocktaking, 46.
Stores, 1, 25, 35.
„ analyses, 69, 71.
Subsist, 11.
Summaries and Analyses, 2, 57, 130, 131.
„ of minerals raised, &c., 57, 131.
Synoptic, 88.

T

TENDERING, sales, 46.
„ stores, 37.

Tendering, work, 19.
Timber measuring, 35.
Time-book, 12.
Time-sheet, 13.
Tin bill, 49.
Tin ore sales, 47, 48, 49.
Transfer book, 114, 120.
„ receipt book, 119.
Transfers, List of, 120.
Transylvania, 23.
Trial balance, 90, 101.
Tribute Account Book, 30.
Tributing, 21.
Truck Acts, 4.
Tutwork, 14, 17.
„ ledger, 30.
„ setting book, 19.

U

UNITED States, 47, 48, 141 (see also *Colorado*).

V

VAN de Linde, G., 50, 51, 53.
Veins, Irregularity of, 103.
Ventilation report, 124.

W

WAGES, Data determining, 11.
„ analysis, 68.
Waste book, 87, 92.
Weigh book, 16, 50.
Weights and Measures, 35, 48.
„ „ Act, 1889, 51.
Workmen, Engagement of, 4.
„ List of, 5, 6, 11.
„ Payment of, 11.

Y

YEARLY Analyses, 131.
„ Reports, 127.

Z

ZINC ore sales, 48.

BELL AND BAIN, LIMITED, PRINTERS, GLASGOW.

www.ingramcontent.com/pod-product-compliance
Lightning Source LLC
Chambersburg PA
CBHW030332170426
43202CB00010B/1103